The Atlas of American Higher Education

THE ATLAS OF AMERICAN HIGHER EDUCATION

James W. Fonseca and Alice C. Andrews

Computer Cartography by Peter J. LaPlaca

New York University Press • New York and London

New York University Press
New York and London

Library of Congress Cataloging-in-Publication Data
Fonseca, James W.
The atlas of American higher education / James W. Fonseca and
Alice C. Andrews ; computer cartography by Peter J. LaPlaca
p.   cm.
Includes bibliographical references (p.) and index.
ISBN 0-8147-2610-0
1. Education, Higher—United States—Maps.   2. Education, Higher—
United States—Statistics.   I. Andrews, Alice C.   II. LaPlaca,
Peter J.   III. Title.   IV. Title: American higher education.
G1201.E68F6   1993 <G&M>
378.73'022'3—dc20   93-522
                         CIP
                         MAP

New York University Press books are printed on acid-free paper,
and their binding materials are chosen for strength and durability.

Manufactured in the United States of America

10   9   8   7   6   5   4   3   2   1

Contents

Acknowledgments

We are grateful to Peter J. LaPlaca, who plotted all the maps in this volume using various computer programs. We would also like to thank Karen Pirhalla who typed the text and Sandy Slater who typed the tables. Vance Grant, Norman Brandt, and Patricia Brown of the National Center for Education Research were particularly helpful. Frank Matthews of *Black Issues in Higher Education* and James Palmer of Illinois State University provided helpful comments.

Many others were helpful in the preparation of the manuscript, maps, statistics, and rankings. They include Tracy Allen, Mary Blackwell, Jimmy Fonseca, Gayle Marcella, Tera Paul, John Prastein, Kimberly Sullivan, Jody Tran, Dan Sydensticker, and William Vaughan. We also thank our editor, Niko Pfund of New York University Press, for his comments and encouragement.

Finally, we are also grateful to our spouses Andy and Elaine, geographer and educator, respectively, for their many helpful comments.

The Atlas of American Higher Education

Introduction

NEED AND PURPOSE

Higher education, as well as K–12 education, is very much on the minds of Americans in this last decade of the twentieth century. We have been characterized as "A Nation at Risk," and our standing compared to other urbanized, industrial countries has been questioned. Education has become a popular and perennial topic in editorial pages and news magazines, and a subject for ceaseless scholarly examination. Because the United States is such a big country, and particularly because our educational system is uniquely divided into fifty state systems, the topic of higher education—as of education in general—needs to be viewed spatially. Not only does public education differ from state to state, but there is an amazing diversity of private institutions in American higher education that also differ from place to place.

A close look at available data quickly reveals that because of this diversity and spatial variation, columns of figures do not tell the whole story. Although some maps essentially reflect the distribution of population (for example, California and New York naturally have the largest enrollments), there are other maps that reflect more complex patterns. These patterns often reflect regional influences in higher education.

Both of us have extensive experience in college teaching and university administration, and are both geographers. James Fonseca holds a Ph.D. in geography, and Alice Andrews an Ed.D. in higher education. We have concluded that there is a need for a series of maps that display various aspects of higher education by state, as well as maps that depict the distribution of various kinds of higher educational institutions. While we hope that this first effort at an atlas of American higher education will find a large audience among interested citizens, we aim it especially at four groups: administrators in colleges and universities, public policymakers involved in higher education at all levels of government, educators in general (especially professors and students in graduate programs of higher education), and geographers (especially teachers and students of cultural geography).

Administrators and public policymakers are concerned with trends and regional patterns in enrollment, finances, minority issues, outcomes, assessment, faculty matters, and student characteristics. The maps allow them to see where their state stands, or on some maps where particular institutions rank, in relation to regional or national peer groups. Professors and students in colleges of education may find the atlas a useful supplement in courses on higher education or teacher education. Finally, we hope the atlas will be of interest to our colleagues who are interested in the cultural and economic geography of the United States, for it contributes to an understanding of the cultural regions of a large and diverse country.

DATA SOURCES

There are a large number of organizations that compile and distribute data on higher education in the United States. To ensure a single standard definition of the various categories of data we have relied primarily on the *Digest of Education Statistics, 1991*, published by the National Center for Education Statistics. This use avoids many definitional problems that might otherwise occur, for example, in defining two-year colleges. Do the data include public and private schools? Senior two-year institutions? Associate degrees granted by four-year colleges? Where necessary, we have utilized other sources such as the *State Higher Education Profiles*, 3d edition (1991), published by the Office of Educational Research and Improvement of the Department of Education, although these data are from 1986–87. Specialized accrediting and professional association sources such as the American Bar Association were used for location maps. All sources for data are cited in the statistical tables in the appendix and in the list of sources. The reader should also be aware that many maps show variation among regions in a single representative year, a "snapshot" rather than long-range regional patterns. This is the case, for example, in the maps of federal agency funding by state for 1988. In creating ratios we have been careful to match dates; for example, 1988 population figures are used to calculate ratios for 1988 enrollment even though 1990 population data are available.

MAPPING OF DATA

The data are displayed on maps drawn by computer-mapping packages. Three standard packages were used: PC-SAS Graphics, ARC-INFO, and Atlas GIS. Different kinds of maps were chosen to portray different kinds of data. The bulk of the data showing quantities and ratios are plotted on choropleth maps. We have tried to keep these maps clear and simple by dividing the data into three categories in most cases, thus giving high, medium, and low ranges. We have chosen intervals that emphasize regional differences and, in many cases, intervals that place roughly equal numbers of states in each category. A map identifying the states is included as map 1.1 in chapter 1. Where the content of the map refers to individual institutions, we have used location maps, sometimes identifying schools by number. For easy reference, the numbers are keyed to lists of schools in the appendix. In some cases, such as in the series of maps of specialized institutions such as law, medical, and veterinary schools, the overall pattern was of primary interest, and it is not possible to identify each institution (more than two hundred in the case of Law Schools, for example). However, these institutions are also listed in tables in the appendix.

Surface maps, where the distribution appears as a topographic surface, were used where a quantity of dollars or population was being mapped. These maps are helpful in determining the relative standing among states as well as in visualizing the overall pattern of a distribution. We have identified important states on each surface map to help orient the reader.

The maps portray the fifty states. Alaska and Hawaii are shown, but not in their real locations or in correct scale. The District of Columbia is not shown on the maps but is cited in the text where warranted, and data for it are included in the appendix. In those cases where it is difficult to determine the choropleth pattern for the small states of Delaware and Rhode Island, we have made mention of their values in the text.

CHAPTER ORGANIZATION

1. Background

This brief chapter provides seven maps that will aid the reader in understanding the remaining maps in the atlas. First is a location map identifying the states. This is followed by six maps of basic demographic data including population, proportion of metropolitan population, African-American population, Hispanic population, and income. Finally, a map showing the location of oldest colleges provides a historical reference point for the development of the American higher education system.

2. Enrollment

Perhaps the most basic measure of American higher education is enrollment—the numbers of students and where they are located. The first series of maps in chapter 2 compares total enrollment to population distribution. In addition to these aggregate measures, we also examine FTE per capita, enrollment growth, and the division of enrollment between public and private colleges. Graduate enrollment is singled out for a closer look in terms of aggregate graduate enrollment, graduate enrollment as a proportion of total enrollment, and the extent of graduate enrollment in private institutions. The final series of maps looks at a number of interrelated measures such as the proportion of part-time students and enrollment of women. Finally, the average enrollment size of public colleges is examined by state.

3. Students and Faculty

While some aspects of the characteristics of students were necessarily covered in chapter 2, others are singled out for treatment in the next section. Of interest are the ratios of college students to population: Which states have the highest ratios? Five maps portray freshmen, the entering higher-education cohort for a specific year; they include a map of the ratio of male to female freshmen and four maps portraying the migration of entering freshmen. This is a topic of interest to state systems that might want to improve their retention of recent graduates from high schools in the state. Other maps show the colleges enrolling the largest numbers of Merit Scholars in 1991 and foreign-student enrollment in the fifty states. A series of five maps shows the percentages of degrees granted in certain fields. They reveal some interesting regional patterns. Last, the faculty-related measures are examined: average faculty salary; female faculty salary as a percentage of male faculty salary; and student-faculty ratios.

4. Cultural Diversity

Minorities in higher education are a topic of increasing importance. They are underrepresented in higher education, and many schools are seeking to improve their recruitment and retention of minority students. Data are available for four groups: African-Americans, Hispanics, Native Americans, and Asians. For each group the share of total enrollment has been mapped. African-American and Hispanic enrollment patterns closely follow population distribution. Native Americans have small enrollment proportions, usually found in states with large Indian reservations. In this chapter, some location maps are used to show the distribution of traditionally black colleges and universities, institutions designated as Hispanic-serving (mostly two-year public institutions), and tribally controlled American Indian colleges.

5. Specialized Institutions

This chapter is different in map style, as it consists entirely of location maps of selected kinds of institutions. Law schools, which are very numerous in our litigious society, are mapped and examined for possible regional patterns. The distribution of three kinds of professional schools in the health-care field are depicted: medical schools, dental schools, and veterinary-medicine schools. The last veterinary school map is of considerable interest. There are a limited number of these schools because of reciprocal agreements among states, and the regional pattern is quite strong. Many kinds of professional schools such as business and nursing schools and theological seminaries have not been chosen for mapping because they are too numerous.

The top research universities, both public and private, as rated by the Carnegie Foundation have been mapped. Other location maps show the sixty largest doctoral-granting institutions and the fifty largest college libraries.

6. Two-Year Colleges

Although two-year colleges represent a huge portion of higher education activity, they are often overlooked or ignored. Our separate section on two-year colleges attempts to give these institutions the emphasis they deserve. In this section we examine overall enrollment, proportion of enrollment in two-year colleges, and average enrollment by college. This is followed by two outcome measures: the number of associate degrees awarded, and a ratio of degrees awarded compared to population. Two maps examine tuition issues: amount of tuition, and community college tuition as a proportion of four-year college tuition. Faculty salaries in two-year colleges are mapped, as are two-year faculty salaries as a proportion of four-year faculty salaries.

7. Outcomes of Higher Education

In this atlas, we have sought to display graphically two kinds of measures of the outcomes of higher education. One is the proportion of adults who have college degrees. This measure is displayed by state, by region, and for different subsets of the population by region (men, women, blacks, and Hispanics). The other measure is the number of various kinds of degrees awarded in a given year related to the total population of states (for example, number of bachelor's degrees per 10,000 population).

8. Student Costs and Student Aid

Here we examine financial issues from the perspective of the student. We examine total costs at public and at private colleges and give a separate examination of tuition costs. Public-college costs are mapped as a proportion of private-college costs, an issue of great interest to students and the families of students choosing between these two options. To help pay these costs a number of student aid programs are offered. Total state spending for aid per student has been mapped, as have grants to students as a proportion of state appropriations for higher education.

9. Financing of Higher Education

Here we look at financial issues not from the perspective of the student, but from the perspective of the state or federal agency appropriating the funds. The first three maps look at state-financing issues. These include maps of expenditures by states for higher education, state appropriations per FTE student, the proportion of state budgets spent on higher education, and recent increases in higher-education expenditures. At the federal level a map of total federal funding is examined. Revenues from federal grants and contracts per faculty member are mapped, and institutions with the largest endowments are also mapped. Finally, the universities receiving the most federal funding for research and development are shown.

10. Summary

In this final chapter, the previous sections are summarized and two additional maps are presented. First is a map showing the extent to which various states have undertaken mandatory outcomes assessment programs. The second map is a composite index measuring the combined weights of eleven of the more important variables.

1

Background

In this chapter we introduce the reader to basic geographic facts necessary for an understanding of the patterns of American higher education discussed in the rest of the atlas. This section consists of seven maps. The first is a simple location map orienting the reader to the locations of the states referred to. The second is a map showing the relative population sizes of the fifty states. The map is a surface map, one that portrays values as a topographic surface in which the "peaks" are in proportion to amount of population. A map of the proportion of each state's population in metropolitan areas follows. This map is useful in the discussions of a number of other maps, including those on part-time enrollment and enrollment of women, among others.

The next two background maps focus on two minority groups, African-Americans and Hispanics. The two maps, showing the proportion of each minority to the population as a whole, will be used in conjunction with several other maps, particularly those in the section on cultural diversity. "Median Household Income," the next map, provides insights in conjunction with a number of maps including those on tuition, educational attainment, and cultural diversity. The last map, on the oldest colleges, provides historical background that is important to understanding the pattern of location of the more established—and often heavily endowed and Ivy League—eastern colleges and universities.

1.1 U.S. LOCATION MAP

This map simply shows the location of all fifty states identified by standard postal abbreviations. The map will help orient the reader to the text and tables contained in this volume.

1.1 U.S. LOCATION MAP

ME

VT NH MA CT RI

NY

PA NJ MD DE D.C.

WV VA

OH KY NC

MI IN TN SC

IL AL GA

WI MO AR FL

MN IA MS LA

ND SD NB KS OK TX

MT WY CO NM HI

ID UT AZ

WA OR NV CA AK

9

1.2 U.S. POPULATION BY STATE

The close correlation between total enrollment and population is clear when this map is compared with map 2.1. This population "surface" map provides one an opportunity to visualize the distribution of the almost 250,000,000 people in the United States as a topographic surface. Most prominent are population peaks in the Northeast, the Midwest, and in the Sunbelt states of Florida, Texas, and California. The largest number of people in a single state, almost 30,000,000, reside in California. The smallest number, 470,000, live in Wyoming. Generally all the states from the Great Plains to the Rocky Mountains, with the exception of Texas, have smaller populations than most states east of the Great Plains. Idaho, Montana, Wyoming, and North and South Dakota form a large area of particularly sparse population in the northern Rocky Mountains and northern Great Plains. Alaska, Maine, New Hampshire, and Vermont and the small states of Rhode Island and Delaware also have small populations.

1.2 U.S. POPULATION BY STATE, 1990

CA NY NJ PA OH NC MI IL GA FL TX

11

1.3 METROPOLITAN AREA POPULATION

Highly urbanized states are the older, often smaller states of Megalopolis along the eastern seaboard, such as Connecticut, Maryland, New Jersey (at 100%, the nation's most urbanized state), and some industrial states of the Midwest, such as Illinois. "Megalopolis," a term coined by the French geographer Jean Gottmann, includes the urbanized strip of cities from Boston to Washington. With their satellite cities and suburbs, the strip includes all or much of the states of New Hampshire, Massachusetts, Rhode Island, Connecticut, New York, New Jersey, Pennsylvania, Delaware, Maryland, and Virginia as well as the District of Columbia. Other highly urbanized states are those where massive and recent in-migration has caused the explosive growth of a large number of urban areas, as in California, Texas, and Florida. Heavy urbanization has also occurred in some western states, where a harsh physical geographical environment has kept population out of rural areas and concentrated it in a few rapidly growing cities. This is the case in Nevada, New Mexico, and Arizona.

1.3 METROPOLITAN AREA POPULATION
(PERCENTAGE OF STATE POPULATION, 1990)

PERCENT

LESS THAN 50

50 TO 80

MORE THAN 80

1.4 AFRICAN-AMERICAN POPULATION

A map showing the distribution of the African-American population is useful in this introductory section, as it is a reference point for several other maps in the "Cultural Diversity" and "Outcomes" chapters. The percentage of African-Americans in the total population is shown by state, using 1990 census figures. The striking feature is the regionalization of the states with large proportions of African-Americans. Except for New York, all the states with over 15 percent are clustered in a compact group south of the old Mason-Dixon line that formed the border between Maryland and Pennsylvania. The region with high percentages stretches from Maryland and Delaware to Louisiana and Arkansas. Florida and Texas, which appear prominently on the next map showing the Hispanic population, fall into the middle category. Also in the 10 to 15 percent category are Missouri, Illinois, Ohio, and Michigan. Although Missouri was originally a slave state, the other three midwestern states, like New York, acquired their urban African-American populations through the northward migrations that began around the time of World War I and continued for many decades.

Among the states, Mississippi ranks highest in terms of its proportion of African-Americans, with nearly 36 percent. However, the District of Columbia, an urban anomaly, is even higher, with nearly 66 percent. Other states in which one-fifth or more of the population is African-American are Louisiana (about 31%), South Carolina (about 30%), Georgia (27%), Alabama (over 25%), Maryland (almost 25%), and North Carolina (22%). Virginia, Tennessee, Delaware, and Arkansas complete the southern tier of high-percentage states. New York, the only northern state in the over-15 percent category, had 15.9 percent in 1990. This represented an increase in the black proportion of the population in New York; in 1980, its percentage was less than 14, and it would not have been in the high category. The West appears as a strikingly large region of less than 10 percent African-American population, as do New England and several other states. To be sure, there are large black populations in many cities, but overall percentages range from 9.2 in Pennsylvania down to 0.3 in Vermont, Idaho, and Montana. California, although it has some large urban African-American minorities, has an overall percentage of 7.4.

1.4 AFRICAN-AMERICAN POPULATION
(PERCENT AFRICAN-AMERICAN, 1990)

PERCENT

LESS THAN 10

10 TO 15

MORE THAN 15

1.5 HISPANIC POPULATION

The Hispanic population of the United States is concentrated along the U.S. border with Mexico, in Florida, in New York City, and in certain other urban areas. The map, which shows the percentage of Hispanics by state reported by the 1990 census, reflects this established pattern. The highest category, over 12 percent Hispanic, includes all of the Mexican border states and Colorado, Florida, and New York. The southwestern states derive their Hispanic population from Mexico, while the Florida Hispanic population is largely Cuban, with a considerable number of recent migrants also from Central America. New York, although it has Hispanics from many sources, gains its large percentage primarily from Puerto Rican migrants. One state, New Mexico, is far ahead of all others in the proportion of Hispanic population; by 1990 it was nearly 40 percent Hispanic. Two more, California and Texas, are over one-fourth Hispanic, and Arizona is not far behind with nearly one-fifth. Colorado, New York, and Florida are all about 12 percent.

In addition to New York, the urban states that have significant proportions of Hispanics are New Jersey, Illinois, Connecticut, Massachusetts, and Rhode Island. Expansion from the border states has carried migrants all the way to the Canadian border in Washington, Oregon, and Idaho, as well as to Wyoming and Kansas. Interestingly, Nevada has over 10 percent, while neighboring Utah has less than 5 percent. The Pacific states of Hawaii and Alaska both fall into the middle category.

The rest of the country, comprising twenty-nine of the fifty states, has less than 3 percent Hispanic population. These states include the South, all of the Midwest except Illinois, and a group of Great Plains states.

1.5 HISPANIC POPULATION
(PERCENT HISPANIC, 1990)

PERCENT

LESS THAN 3

3 TO 12

MORE THAN 12

1.6 MEDIAN HOUSEHOLD INCOME

The map displays the distribution of median household income, an explanatory variable that is useful in understanding many of the other maps. It is especially appropriate to use it when looking at chapter 7 on the outcomes of the higher educational process, and chapters 8 and 9 on student costs and financing. One might expect some correspondence between affluence, as measured by median household income, and educational attainment, as depicted by the proportion of adults with four years of college. It might also be logical to assume that states where households have high annual income may invest more heavily in higher education.

Highest median household incomes (more than $30,000) are found in a belt of East Coast states extending from New Hampshire to Virginia. Three Midwest states also fall in the high category— Illinois, Michigan, and Minnesota. In the West there are five states in the over $30,000 category; they are Hawaii, Alaska, Washington, California, and Utah. There are nineteen states in the middle category, with median household incomes in the $25,000 to $30,000 range. There is no regional pattern in this category; these states are distributed throughout the country. In the lowest category, less than $25,000, ten of the thirteen states lie in the southern tier, mostly in the Southeast, but New Mexico is also included. The other three are South Dakota, Montana, and Idaho.

1.6 MEDIAN HOUSEHOLD INCOME, 1990

DOLLARS

LESS THAN 25,000

25,000 TO 30,000

MORE THAN 30,000

1.7 OLDEST COLLEGES

Colleges founded before 1800 in the original thirteen states and in adjacent areas settled in the colonial period have been mapped here. Only three had been founded by 1700. Harvard was founded in Cambridge, Massachusetts, in 1636, establishing a model for church-related colleges designed primarily to educate young men for the ministry. The College of William and Mary in Williamsburg, Virginia, was founded in 1693, and St. John's College in Annapolis, Maryland (which was originally called King William's School), was founded in 1696. Only six colleges were founded in the first half of the eighteenth century. Yale was founded in Connecticut in 1701, and the others were all founded in the 1740's. The first two were in Pennsylvania—the University of Pennsylvania in Philadelphia in 1740 and Moravian College in Bethlehem in 1742. The University of Delaware was founded in Newark in 1743 and Princeton in New Jersey in 1746. The first school in the interior was established in the Great Valley of Virginia in 1749; it bore several names before finally evolving into the present Washington and Lee University.

The next fifty years saw the founding of many institutions of higher education, some twenty-nine in all. The second half of this period, after the signing of the Declaration of Independence, saw a particularly rapid increase in the number of colleges; 21 were founded in the period 1776–98. It also saw a change in the distribution pattern. The first three colleges had been located on the coast and five of the next six were not far inland, but by 1800 the frontier had moved westward. Opportunities for higher education moved with it. New colleges were founded in northern New England, as far north as Maine and northern Vermont, and also in the interior in southern states like North Carolina and Georgia. More remarkably, new colleges were founded in the frontier areas of Tennessee and Kentucky. Transylvania College was founded in Kentucky in 1780, and the forerunner of the University of Louisville was established in 1798.

1.7 OLDEST COLLEGES
(FOUNDED BEFORE 1800)

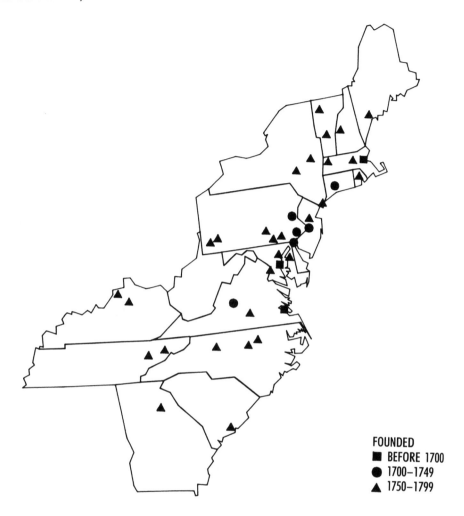

FOUNDED
■ BEFORE 1700
● 1700–1749
▲ 1750–1799

2

Enrollment

2.1 TOTAL ENROLLMENT

Enrollment is concentrated in the more populous states of the Northeast and Midwest, and in California, Florida, and Texas. Enrollments in 1989 ranged from a high of 1,745,000 students in California to fewer than 30,000 in Alaska and Wyoming. The map of enrollment shows a great deal of correspondence with the map of population in chapter 1. This is to be expected, not only because the more populous states have more students, but also because the vast majority of students remain in their home states to get their college education—81 percent on average in the United States, and as high as 92 percent in several states. In fact, self-sufficiency was an implied goal for some states in the 1960s. So closely are enrollment and population related that the eight states with total enrollments of 500,000 or more are the same eight states with the largest populations. These eight, in order of enrollment (population rank in parentheses) are California (1), New York (2), Texas (3), Illinois (6), Pennsylvania (5), Florida (4), Michigan (8), and Ohio (7). Five of these populous states are in the Midwest and Northeast; the other three are in the Sunbelt. At the other end of the scale, those states with the lowest total enrollments, fewer than 100,000 students, are the states with small populations. Fourteen of the nation's states with the smallest populations are among the sixteen states that have fewer than 100,000 students. Two clusters of these are the three states in northern New England, and the five states in the northern Rocky Mountains and northern Great Plains. The map of total enrollment is thus largely a map of population distribution

2.1 TOTAL ENROLLMENT
(ALL INSTITUTIONS OF HIGHER EDUCATION, FALL 1989)

STUDENTS

LESS THAN 100,000

100,001 TO 250,000

250,001 TO 500,000

MORE THAN 500,000

2.2 FTE ENROLLMENT PER 1,000 POPULATION

This map shows full-time equivalent (FTE) enrollment per 1,000 population. It is a measure of the proportion of a state's residents attending college, although students from one state attending school out-of-state are counted in the state in which they attend college. So this map is only an approximate measure of the proportion of one state's residents attending schools. New Jersey, for example, with its very large proportion of students leaving to attend schools out-of-state, falls in the lowest category. Massachusetts on the other hand, with its large attraction of out-of-state students, falls in the highest category.

In general, there is a tendency for states of the North and West to have higher enrollment figures per 1,000 than in the South. Except for Delaware, Virginia, North Carolina, Alabama, and Oklahoma, all southern states fall in the lowest category, with fewer than 39 FTE per 1,000 capita. Three of the five states with the lowest ratios (although not the two very lowest states) are in the South: Arkansas, Florida, and Georgia, all with ratios of 29 or 30. Nevada and New Jersey have the lowest ratio, 28. Other nonsouthern states with low ratios are Maine, Alaska, and Hawaii.

States in the highest category, more than 45 FTE per capita, include three New England states (Massachusetts, Rhode Island, and Vermont) as well as five states in the north-central part of the country (Wisconsin, Iowa, Nebraska, Kansas, and North Dakota). In the West, Utah is the only state in the highest category. The highest ratios are in Rhode Island and Massachusetts, 58 and 55, respectively—more than twice the ratio of the lowest state, Nevada. Although not shown on the map, the District of Columbia has the highest ratio of FTE per 1,000, 103. States in the intermediate category, 39 to 45 FTE per 1,000, are clustered in the northern half of the country.

2.2 FTE ENROLLMENT PER 1,000 POPULATION, FALL 1989

RATIO

LESS THAN 39

39 TO 45

MORE THAN 45

2.3 ENROLLMENT GROWTH

Just as enrollment mirrors population distribution, enrollment growth, as measured by the percentage change in enrollment from fall 1980 to fall 1989, largely reflects population growth. Many of the Sunbelt states have experienced large enrollment gains, while the Snowbelt states have experienced slow growth or enrollment decreases. So closely does enrollment growth mirror population growth that of the eleven states that experienced enrollment growth of at least 24 percent, eight are also among the states leading in population growth as measured by at least a 10 percent gain between 1980 and 1990. Only two states, Alabama and Wyoming, had large gains in enrollment without a corresponding increase in population. Alabama grew by only 4 percent in population and Wyoming actually lost 3 percent of its population between 1980 and 1990, yet both absorbed an increase of more than 20 percent in students. Maine, the third state of the eleven, grew by 9.6 percent. On the other hand, a few states had relatively large population increases over the decade without corresponding increases in enrollment. California's population grew by 26 percent, Washington's by 18 percent, and South Carolina's by 12 percent, yet all four states had enrollment increases below 12 percent.

Many states had minimal population growth or even population loss, and predictably, a corresponding low rate of growth in enrollment. Many states of the Northeast and Midwest were in this category. West Virginia had a population loss of 7.6 percent; Pennsylvania, Illinois, and Michigan all grew by less than one percent. All of these states had less than 12 percent growth in enrollment.

The correlation between population growth and enrollment is not perfect, of course, because a number of other factors intervene. A state may grow in population but experience an increase in the proportion of students attending out-of-state schools. The rate of high school graduates going or not going to college may change. The demographic composition of the population growth also has an important impact. For example, an influx of older residents will not result in an increase in college enrollment. Overall, however, in the eight-year time interval examined, national enrollment grew by 8.6 percent, or almost 250,000 students—the equivalent of fifty new mid-size universities of 5,000 students in just nine years!

2.3 ENROLLMENT GROWTH
(PERCENT CHANGE, FALL 1980 TO FALL 1989)

PERCENT

LESS THAN 12

12 TO 24

MORE THAN 24

2.4 ENROLLMENT IN PUBLIC COLLEGES

Enrollment in public institutions totaled 10,515,000 students in 1989, or 78 percent of American higher-education enrollment. Predictably the pattern largely mirrors population distribution, with the largest enrollments in the Northeast and the Midwest and in the states of California, Texas, and Florida. Virginia and North Carolina also stand out because of fairly large populations combined with a smaller than average proportion of enrollment in private colleges and universities. As with other population-related maps, the lowest enrollments in public institutions are in the northern Rocky Mountain and northern Great Plains states, northern New England, Alaska, and small states such as Delaware and Rhode Island. The two states at the far ends of the range of enrollment are California with 1,543,000 students in public colleges and universities, and South Dakota with 25,000 students.

2.4 ENROLLMENT IN PUBLIC COLLEGES, FALL 1989

STUDENTS

LESS THAN 125,000

125,000 TO 250,000

MORE THAN 250,000

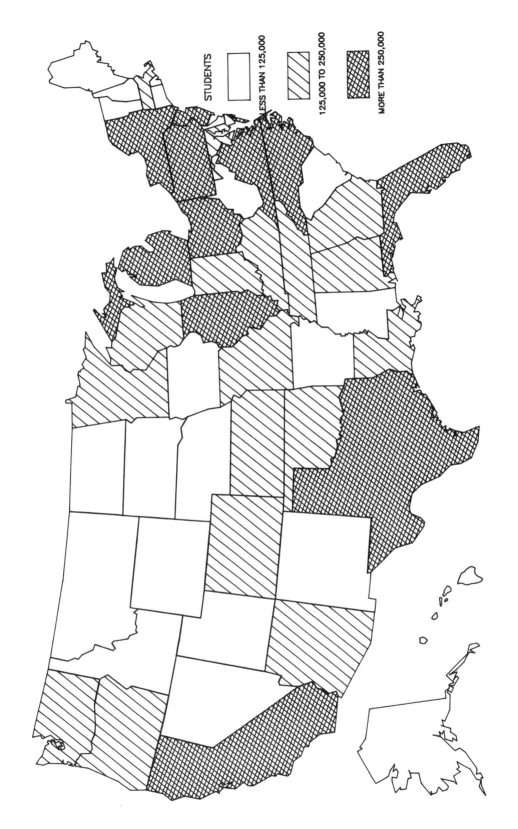

2.5 ENROLLMENT IN PRIVATE COLLEGES

The distribution of enrollment in private colleges does not follow general patterns of population distribution as closely as some other variables do. There is much more of an east-west orientation to this map, reflecting the large number of private institutions in the earlier-settled eastern states. Of the twenty-nine states with at least 25,000 students enrolled in private institutions, all but five (California, Texas, Washington, Colorado, and Utah) are east of the Great Plains. In the eastern half of the country, those states with fewer than 25,000 students in private colleges are generally those states with small populations such as Delaware, West Virginia, two states of northern New England, and a cluster of three states in the South: Arkansas, Mississippi, and Alabama.

The concentration of private enrollment in the East can be seen readily through comparison with California's enrollment totals. On almost all other absolute measures of enrollment, California, the most populous state, stands out (almost 30,000,000 people compared to second-place New York's 18,000,000 people). But California's 211,000 students in private universities are fewer than those in Massachusetts (239,000) or Pennsylvania (275,000), and essentially half those of New York (418,000). In fact, the five states of Massachusetts, New York, Pennsylvania, Ohio, and Illinois have 1,243,000 private college students, 42 percent of the national total. In addition, three large private eastern universities (Northeastern University, New York University, and Boston University) each have larger student bodies than the total private enrollments in each of the twenty-one states that have fewer than 25,000 students enrolled in private colleges.

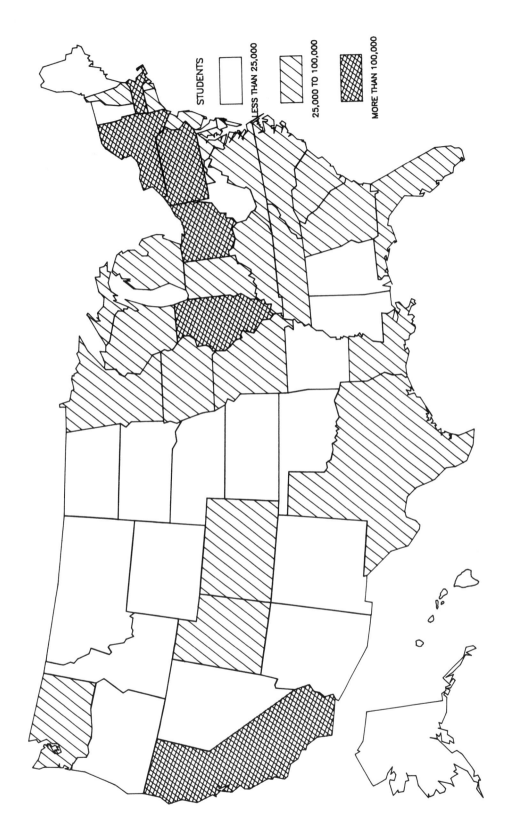

2.5 ENROLLMENT IN PRIVATE COLLEGES, FALL 1989

STUDENTS

LESS THAN 25,000

25,000 TO 100,000

MORE THAN 100,000

2.6 PROPORTION OF ENROLLMENT IN PRIVATE FOUR-YEAR COLLEGES

There is a wide range in the proportion of undergraduate enrollment in private and public four-year colleges. The proportion ranges from zero in Wyoming, the only state with no private four-year colleges, and one percent in Nevada, to 67 percent in Massachusetts. Although not shown on the map, the District of Columbia has an even higher percentage, 84 percent; its only public four-year institution is the University of the District of Columbia. But the district has fifteen private colleges and universities—some of them old and distinguished, such as Georgetown University—offering at least a bachelor's degree.

The map reveals some striking regional groupings. There are two blocs of states in which private colleges account for more than 40 percent of total four-year enrollment. The first is in the Northeast and includes Pennsylvania, New York, and all of the New England states except Maine. Besides Massachusetts, Rhode Island and New York are the only states in which the number of students enrolled in private institutions is larger than the number in public institutions. New Hampshire is evenly split at 50 percent. Throughout the states in this northeastern bloc, the tradition of private education has been strong. Many of the colleges are old, with Harvard, the oldest, dating from 1636. Public systems of higher education were comparatively late in appearing, particularly in Massachusetts, and faced entrenched competition from the established private schools.

The second bloc consists of Iowa, Missouri, and Illinois, all with 41 to 46 percent private enrollment. Illinois includes such noted private universities as the University of Chicago and Northwestern University as well as many smaller schools. Missouri's premier private institution is Washington University in St. Louis, but it has a total of fifty-one private four-year colleges and only thirteen public ones.

A few other states also have a relatively large percentage of enrollment in private schools (25%–40%). They are mostly in the East and include the remaining northeastern states and Ohio, Virginia, Tennessee, North Carolina, and Florida. West of the Mississippi, only five states fall into this middle category: Minnesota, Utah, Washington, California, and Hawaii. Because of its Mormon heritage, Utah stands out among western states in this regard, as it does in almost any other demographic variable. Thirty-nine percent of its undergraduates are enrolled in private institutions, with Brigham Young University being the chief institution of higher learning in the Mormon region.

The remaining western states, the Plains states, and the Deep South have a small proportion of private enrollment, less than 25 percent. Also included in this low category are Wisconsin, Indiana, Michigan, Kentucky, and West Virginia.

PERCENT

LESS THAN 25

25 TO 40

MORE THAN 40

* NOT APPLICABLE

2.7 GRADUATE AND FIRST PROFESSIONAL ENROLLMENT

The 1,792,000 graduate and first professional school students (law, medicine, veterinary, etc.) account for 13 percent of total enrollment. The bulk of that enrollment is accounted for by graduate students; professional students account for only 15 percent of the graduate and first professional total. These two categories of enrollment are concentrated in the Midwest and Northeast and in a few other large states such as California and Texas. As was shown on the map of private college enrollment, graduate enrollments tend to be concentrated in the earlier-settled northeastern part of the nation. A band of states in the North (including Illinois, Michigan, Ohio, Pennsylvania, New York, and Massachusetts) accounts for 604,000 of the nation's graduate and first professional students, one-third of the national total. As with private university enrollment, California does not dominate graduate and first professional enrollment as one might expect from its sheer population size. Even though California has more than 11,000,000 more people than New York, its graduate enrollment of 198,000 is only slightly higher than New York's 190,000. Texas also has a substantial number of graduate students: 111,000. In total, the eight states mentioned above have more than 60 percent of the nation's graduate students.

As the map of graduate enrollment at least partly reflects population, the eastern states tend to have larger enrollments, with the exception of states with smaller populations such as those in northern New England and Rhode Island, Delaware, and West Virginia. In turn, western states with smaller populations, particularly those in the northern Rocky Mountains and northern Great Plains, have limited graduate enrollments. In fact, large campuses in the northeastern states or in California or Texas often have more graduate students than whole states in these less populated regions. Wyoming, Montana, Alaska, Nevada, and both Dakotas each have fewer than 5,000 graduate and first professional students.

2.7 GRAPHATE AND FIRST PROFESSIONAL ENROLLMENT, FALL 1989

STUDENTS

LESS THAN 20,000

20,001 TO 40,000

40,001 TO 60,000

MORE THAN 60,000

2.8 GRADUATE ENROLLMENT AS A PROPORTION OF TOTAL ENROLLMENT

The map of graduate and first professional enrollment as a proportion of total enrollment shows that a cluster of several eastern states—Massachusetts, Connecticut, New York, New Jersey, Pennsylvania, Maryland, and Virginia—have the highest proportions of graduate enrollment. This reflects the earlier settlement of the East and the fact that it takes longer to develop graduate programs than it does to establish community college or four-year programs. These states have a concentration of older established universities with large endowments and connections to research funding that are critical to the support of graduate students. In addition to these northeastern states, a cluster of three states in the interior of the country, made up of Missouri, Iowa, and Illinois, also has more than 13 percent of its enrollment accounted for by graduate students. Four southern states are also in this category: South Carolina, Georgia, Louisiana, and Oklahoma.

These fourteen states are relatively specialized in graduate enrollment. The most specialized are the District of Columbia (not shown on map) (38%); Connecticut (21%); Massachusetts (20%); and New York (19%). As a comparison with the next map will show, private university enrollment plays an important part in allowing these states to specialize in graduate education. Six of the eight states with more than 50 percent of their graduate enrollment in private schools are among these fourteen states with high overall graduate enrollment.

States with a small ratio of graduate enrollment to total enrollment are also clustered in a few areas. A few southern states including Florida, Mississippi, and Arkansas are in this category. A second cluster is in the northern Great Plains and northern Rocky Mountain states, and an adjacent cluster is in the states of the Great Basin including Utah, Nevada, and Arizona. All the other states in the lowest category, less than 11 percent, are quite scattered: Maine, Wisconsin, Washington, and Alaska. The lowest proportions of graduate enrollment are in the West, especially in Alaska, Utah, and Nevada.

States in the intermediate category, 11 to 13 percent, are concentrated in a few large clusters: the largest is a bloc of six states focused on Colorado, New Mexico, and the adjacent Great Plains states from Texas to South Dakota (excluding Oklahoma). A second cluster is located in the eastern Midwest, spilling over to Kentucky, Tennessee, and North Carolina. A third is in the West: California, Oregon, and Idaho. Three New England states also fall into this category: Vermont, New Hampshire, and Rhode Island.

It should be noted that the intervals on this map are closely spaced, with the highest category, more than 13 percent, only two percentage points higher than the lowest category, less than 11 percent. Yet, as we have seen, there are distinct regional patterns. In addition, the differences among states at the upper and lower ends are wide: for example, Connecticut's 21 percent compared to Alaska's 4 percent in proportion of enrollment at the graduate level.

2.8 GRADUATE ENROLLMENT AS A PROPORTION OF TOTAL ENROLLMENT, FALL 1989

PERCENT

LESS THAN 11

11 TO 13

MORE THAN 13

2.9 PRIVATE GRADUATE ENROLLMENT AS A PROPORTION OF TOTAL GRADUATE ENROLLMENT

There are only a few states where enrollment in private graduate and first professional schools makes up the majority of total graduate enrollment. These states are concentrated in the Northeast, including Massachusetts, New Hampshire, Vermont, Connecticut, New York, and Pennsylvania. There is a second cluster of two states in Illinois and Missouri. The District of Columbia stands out as having 97 percent of its graduate enrollment in private schools. This is to be expected, since the only public university is the University of the District of Columbia and there is a large number of private schools with substantial graduate enrollment, including Georgetown, George Washington, Catholic, American, and Howard universities. Among the fifty states, Massachusetts is highest with 77 percent private graduate enrollment, followed by New Hampshire (66%) and New York (65%). These eight states and the District of Columbia have more than half (53%) of all private graduate enrollments.

East of the Great Plains, the remaining states are divided between the intermediate category (20%–50% private graduate enrollment) and the lowest category (less than 20% private graduate enrollment). It is to the west of the Great Plains that graduate and first professional enrollment in public universities becomes overwhelmingly concentrated. The three Pacific Coast states and Colorado and Utah are in the intermediate category, and all the remaining states of the Great Plains and West are in the lowest category. In large part this reflects the more recent settlement of these states and the fact that educational systems were established at the time of the land-grant schools and later, when public education was the predominant mode. Two of these states, Wyoming and Nevada, have no private graduate or first professional enrollment. Four others—Kansas, New Mexico, Montana, and North Dakota—have less than 5 percent private graduate enrollment, indicating the presence of very few private universities and even fewer that offer graduate work. New Mexico, for example, has only two private schools offering master's work, the College of Santa Fe and St. John's College. Nationally, 39 percent of graduate enrollment is in private universities.

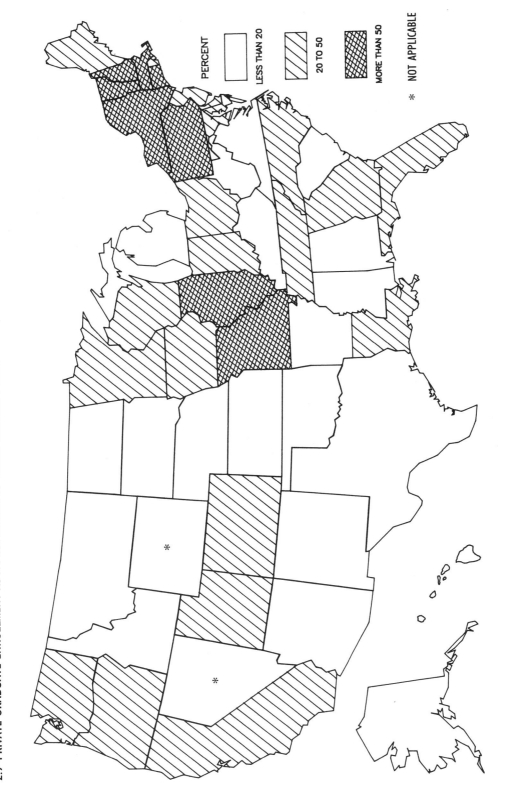

2.9 PRIVATE GRADUATE ENROLLMENT AS A PROPORTION OF TOTAL GRADUATE ENROLLMENT, FALL 1989

PERCENT

LESS THAN 20

20 TO 50

MORE THAN 50

* NOT APPLICABLE

2.10 PART-TIME STUDENTS AS A PROPORTION OF TOTAL ENROLLMENT

The map of proportion of part-time enrollment shows a concentration of states with more than 44 percent part-time enrollment in a band of western states from California to Texas. A few states in the Megalopolis strip also stand out, as do Florida, Michigan, Illinois, and Alaska. States with the smallest proportion of part-time enrollment, less than 36 percent, tend to be concentrated in two areas: the northern Rocky Mountain states and the Dakotas, and a broad band of southern states from Arkansas to South Carolina.

There is a strong geographical factor to this pattern. Most part-time college students are urban residents, holding down a job during the day and taking classes on evenings or weekends. To a large extent, the map thus reflects the level of urbanization among the states (see map 1.3, "Metropolitan Area Population," in chapter 1).

The correlation between a large proportion of part-time enrollment and a high degree of urbanization is not perfect, but it is substantial. Eleven of the twelve states with more than 44 percent part-time students are also among the nation's most highly urbanized states. Alaska and Maine are the only exceptions. These states are only 41 percent and 36 percent urbanized, respectively, and yet have a large part-time student population, perhaps reflecting the part-time economy of much of both states.

Three highly urbanized states (all over 90% urban) do not stand out in the proportion of part-time students: Massachusetts, New York, and Rhode Island. Here the large number of established universities, many of them private and Ivy League, attract students from all over the country who raise the proportion of full-time students.

At the opposite extreme, states with lower levels of urbanization have large proportions of full-time students. Of the twelve least urbanized states (45% or less metropolitan population), nine appear on the map in the lowest category, with 36 percent or less part-time students. In addition to Alaska and Maine, Wyoming also has a slightly larger proportion of part-time students than expected from its level of urbanization.

Women are very much the majority in part-time enrollment: 58 percent. In forty-nine of the fifty states, women enrolled part-time outnumber men enrolled part-time. The only state where male part-timers outnumber women is Utah, where the cultural influence of the Mormon Church undoubtedly plays a role.

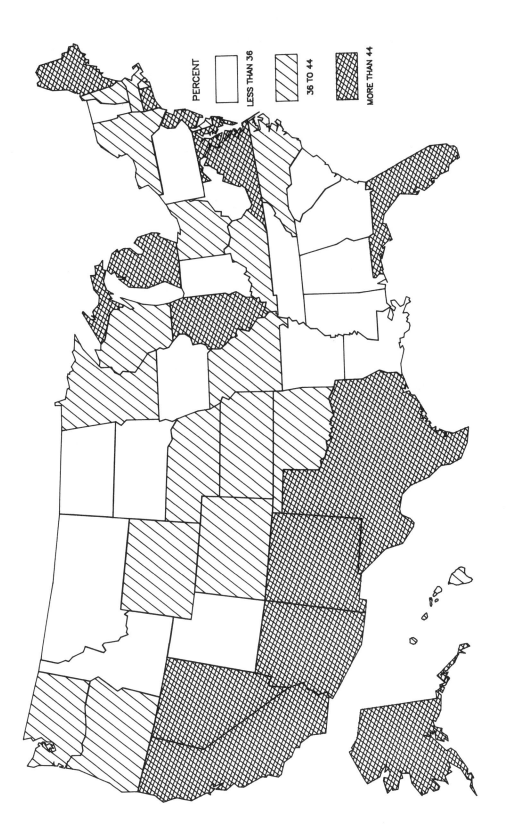

2.10 PART-TIME STUDENTS AS A PROPORTION OF TOTAL ENROLLMENT, FALL 1989

PERCENT

LESS THAN 36

36 TO 44

MORE THAN 44

2.11 FULL-TIME ENROLLMENT MAJORITY: MALE OR FEMALE

Females greatly outnumber males in total college enrollment (full- and part-time). Of the 13,457,855 students enrolled, women account for 54 percent. Yet the ratio of full-time male to full-time female students is much closer. In this category, women have only a slight lead, 51 percent to 49 percent. When a map is made in terms of whether males or females make up the majority of enrollment by state, an interesting east-west dichotomy emerges that partly reflects demography: women generally outnumber men in the eastern half of the country. East of the Mississippi, only two states, Vermont and Indiana, have male majorities. Women make up the majority of full-time enrollment in all states east of the Great Plains with only three exceptions: Iowa, Indiana, and New Hampshire. From the Great Plains to the Pacific, females are the majority in eleven states and males in eight.

This much lower proportion of female full-time enrollment compared to part-time occurs for a variety of reasons. Women are increasingly working outside the home and frequently attend college on a part-time rather than full-time basis. Women who work only in the home may also attend college on a part-time basis. In addition, another major factor is geographical: women make up a relatively larger proportion of the nation's urban population and thus are more likely to be part-time rather than full-time students due to the accessibility afforded by urban universities. A reason for the larger proportion of female population in the East is the general east-to-west trend in migration by males in the nation, which tends to result in more females in the East and more males in the West. In addition to general migration principles, this trend may be true of students leaving home for college as well; perhaps males are more likely than females to be encouraged or to be willing to leave their home states to go to college.

2.11 FULL-TIME ENROLLMENT MAJORITY: MALE OR FEMALE? FALL 1989

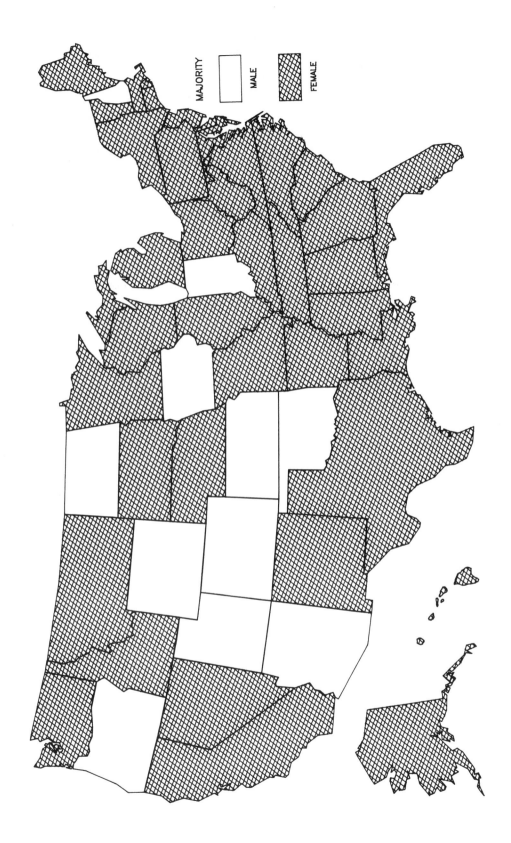

2.12 WOMEN ENROLLED FULL-TIME AS A PROPORTION OF TOTAL ENROLLMENT

As noted on the previous map, while women dominate in total enrollment, full-time enrollment is almost evenly split between men and women. However, that roughly equal division is not spread evenly through the nation; women form the majority of full-time enrollment east of the Great Plains while the ratios on the Great Plains and farther west are more evenly balanced.

The map of the ratio of women enrolled full-time to total enrollment confirms the relationship between urbanization and full-time female students; that is, women in urban areas tend to be part-time students. If map 2.12 is compared with the map of proportion of population in metropolitan areas, map 1.3, a number of connections are evident. Of the eleven states with the highest proportion of full-time women to total enrollment (more than 34%), eight are among the fifteen least urbanized states. The highest ratios of full-time female enrollment to total enrollment are in the three states in the lower Mississippi River basin: Louisiana, Arkansas, and Mississippi, all with ratios between 39 percent and 41 percent. Conversely, of the fourteen most urbanized states, ten fall into the lowest category of full-time women enrolled—less than 31 percent. The other four states—Massachusetts, Rhode Island, Pennsylvania, and New York—singled out previously in terms of proportion of private enrollment and proportion of graduate enrollment, may as a consequence still reflect a male, Ivy League bias in admission or in self-selection by students. The three states with the lowest proportion of full-time female enrollment to total enrollment are Nevada (15%), Alaska (18%), and Arizona (19%).

2.12 WOMEN ENROLLED FULL-TIME AS A PROPORTION OF TOTAL ENROLLMENT, FALL 1989

PERCENT

LESS THAN 31

31 TO 34

MORE THAN 34

2.13 AVERAGE ENROLLMENT AT PUBLIC FOUR-YEAR COLLEGES

Average enrollment size of public four-year colleges varies greatly by state, from more than 32,000 in Arizona to 3,500 in South Dakota. This map divides college sizes into three classes: more than 12,000 students, fewer than 8,000 students, and those in between. The map shows some distinct regional patterns. Large state-college campuses, those averaging 12,000 students or more, are concentrated in Kentucky and the Midwest, and in California, Wyoming, and the Southwest. Only a few other states have large average-sized campuses—Washington, Florida, and Rhode Island. In the last case, only two four-year public institutions are included, the University of Rhode Island and Rhode Island College. Several single campuses with 30,000 or more students in some of the larger states have more students than are enrolled in the entire public college systems of Alaska, South Dakota, Vermont, or Wyoming.

Small average campus size, fewer than 8,000 students, is found in all parts of the country in states with small populations. Of the nation's fifteen states with the smallest populations, eight are represented on the map in the smallest campus category. The smallest average campus size is in South Dakota, where an average of 3,500 students attend each of the state's six public colleges. The corollary proposition, that states with large populations have large average public campus sizes, is generally not true. Of the fifteen most populous states, only five have large average campus size (California, Florida, Illinois, Michigan, and Indiana). Two have small average campus sizes (Pennsylvania and Georgia). The remaining states have medium-sized campuses.

Average campus enrollment is in part related to the number of campuses in a state system. The number of public four-year colleges varies greatly by state, but the most are in Pennsylvania, New York, and Texas, all with from forty to forty-three state colleges. California has thirty-one four-year colleges. At the other extreme, Wyoming has one public four-year college and three states have only two public four-year colleges: Delaware, Nevada, and Rhode Island.

2.13 AVERAGE ENROLLMENT AT PUBLIC FOUR-YEAR COLLEGES, FALL 1989

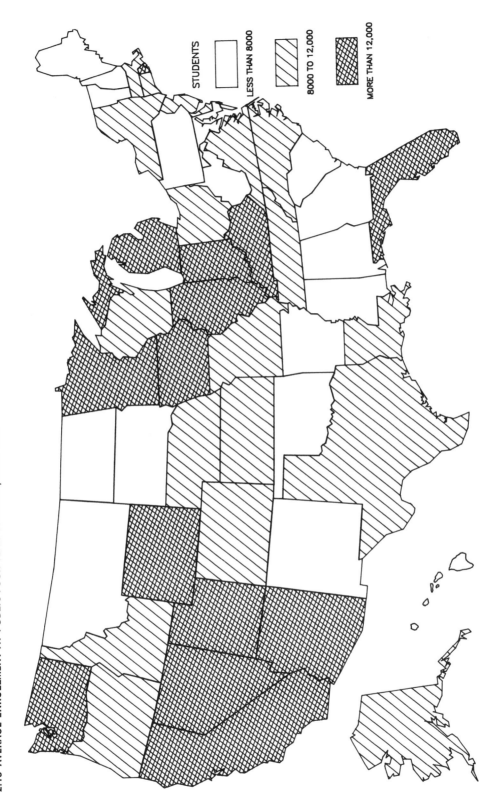

STUDENTS

LESS THAN 8000

8000 TO 12,000

MORE THAN 12,000

3

Students and Faculty

3.1 COLLEGE STUDENTS PER 1,000 POPULATION

One way of indicating the importance of higher education in an area is to map the number of college students per 1,000 population. This is similar to the way that the number of physicians or health-care professionals to population is sometimes mapped to give an indication of the availability of health care. Clearly many factors influence such a ratio of students to population. Most obvious are the number of colleges in the state, the spaces available in them, and the number of prospective students. The number of prospective students is in turn related to basic demographic characteristics such as the age structure of the population. Socioeconomic influences include the income levels in the state, which are in turn related to the occupational structure, the health of the economy, and ethnic composition. All states are not equal; they have different economies, different school systems, and different demographic characteristics.

A ratio of college students to population has been mapped, with some interesting and perhaps surprising results. A large region in the central interior part of the country stands out as having high rates, with an average of more than 60 students per 1,000 population. It extends from Michigan, Wisconsin, and Illinois in the East to Utah and Arizona in the West. Four eastern states (Vermont, Massachusetts, Rhode Island, and Delaware) also have high rates, as does Alabama. At the other end of the scale, the low category of 55 students includes most southern states except Alabama (and Virginia and Maryland, which are in the middle category). It also includes three New England states (Maine, New Hampshire, and Connecticut), some urban/industrial states (New Jersey, Pennsylvania, Ohio, and Indiana), and some western states (South Dakota, Montana, Idaho, Washington, Nevada, Alaska, and Hawaii). Looking at the ranking of states on this measure is helpful. Excluding the anomalous high rate of about 133 students per 1,000 people in the District of Columbia, the rates are fairly closely clustered, ranging from a high of 78 in Rhode Island to a low of 38.5 in Arkansas. Arizona ranks after Rhode Island with 72.2, a not unexpected figure for a state that attracts large numbers of student migrants and in which higher education is almost an industry. Nebraska, with a figure of 71.5, and Utah, with 70.4, come next. The only state other than Arkansas that had a rate lower than 40 per 1,000 in 1990 was Georgia, with 38.5. These two states are quite different: Arkansas has relatively few institutions of higher education, and Georgia has many, including some prestigious ones like Emory and Georgia Tech, as well as a number of notable black schools. To repeat, the map is interesting but difficult to explain. It is easy to understand why Massachusetts has about 70 students per 1,000, more difficult to understand why states like Georgia and Florida, with many schools, have far lower ratios than their neighbor Alabama. Clearly, each state has to be individually analyzed on the basis of all the characteristics mentioned above.

3.1 COLLEGE STUDENTS PER 1,000 POPULATION, 1990

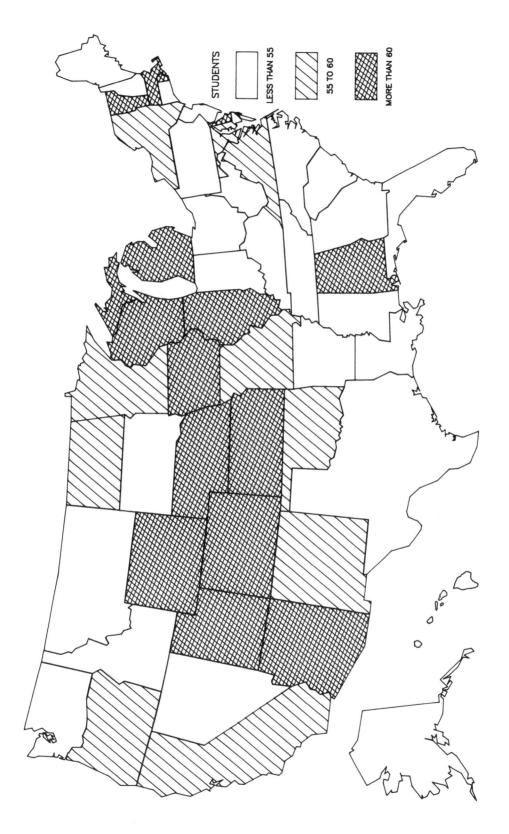

STUDENTS

LESS THAN 55

55 TO 60

MORE THAN 60

3.2 SEX RATIO OF ENTERING FRESHMEN

As a standard demographic measure, the sex ratio of a population is the number of males per 100 females; it is useful in many international and regional comparisons. In the United States, the sex ratio has traditionally been higher in the West, fitting in with the ideas of the frontier and of rural, dispersed populations. Mapping the sex ratio of entering college freshmen produces a rather interesting regional pattern.

On this map, based on 1988 figures, males predominate only in the single state of Vermont in the East and in six interior states in the western census region. These include North Dakota and Kansas in the Great Plains, the mountain states of Wyoming and Colorado, and the southwestern states of Arizona and New Mexico. No general conclusions can be drawn, however, for next door to North Dakota, South Dakota falls into the lowest category, with fewer than 90 males per 100 females, as do Montana, Idaho, and Utah, all bordering states with high sex ratios.

A more discernible region is the South, where a low sex ratio of fewer than 90 males per 100 females prevails in a bloc of states extending from Delaware south through Georgia and west across the Mississippi to include Louisiana, Arkansas, and Missouri. Also in the low category are Massachusetts, New York, New Jersey, and Michigan, as well as Alaska and Hawaii. The largest number of states, twenty-three in all, fall into this low category.

In the remaining twenty states, the sex ratio falls between 90 and 100. For the United States as a whole, the sex ratio among entering freshmen in 1988 was 91 males per 100 females.

3.2 SEX RATIO OF ENTERING FRESHMEN
(NUMBER OF MALES PER 100 FEMALES, FALL 1988)

STUDENTS

LESS THAN 90

90 TO 100

MORE THAN 100

3.3 PROPORTION OF IN-STATE FRESHMEN

The next four maps attempt to give a picture of residence and migration patterns among entering college freshmen, specifically those attending four-year colleges. Such students are likely to be making moves, "going away to college," while the freshmen entering two-year colleges, many of which are community colleges, are more likely to stay in their own communities. The freshman classes of four-year colleges may also contain adults entering college, often after many years have elapsed since their high school graduations; they usually go to local colleges.

The first map shows the proportion of in-state freshmen among recent high school graduates attending four-year colleges. This may be a meaningful measure of how many potential students are retained in their home state. The map is striking in that it shows that less than 75 percent of freshmen in New England and New York are from in-state. Yet New England and New York have many colleges, including many of the most prestigious in the country. Student migration from other states into New England is playing a role in depressing the percentage of in-state residents in that area. Also in this low category is Delaware. Many students will travel several hours away from home in order to go to college, so they are more likely to cross state boundaries in small states than in large. The New England states and Delaware fall into this category. Also, many freshmen are part-time and commuting students. Such students are more likely to cross state boundaries in commuting to colleges in the heavily urbanized northeastern seaboard. The commuting fields for Boston, New York, Philadelphia, and Washington, D.C., all include parts of several states. Other states in which the proportion of in-state freshmen is less than 75 percent are the two Dakotas, Utah, and Idaho. These are large states in which the commuting-field rationale clearly does not apply.

Fourteen states, including Hawaii, fall into the highest category, with more than 85 percent of freshmen being in-state residents. In the case of Hawaii, distance and isolation are deterrents to extensive student migration either in or out. Eight other states in the high-resident category are west of the Mississippi. Illinois (ranking first with 92%), Michigan, and Ohio, all with large and prestigious state systems, also fall into the high category. The only state on the East Coast that has more than 85 percent in-state freshmen is New Jersey; in this case the large percentage is explained by the heavy out-migration of students, as shown on the next maps. Twenty-three states fall into the intermediate category, with 75 to 85 percent of their freshmen students being in-state residents.

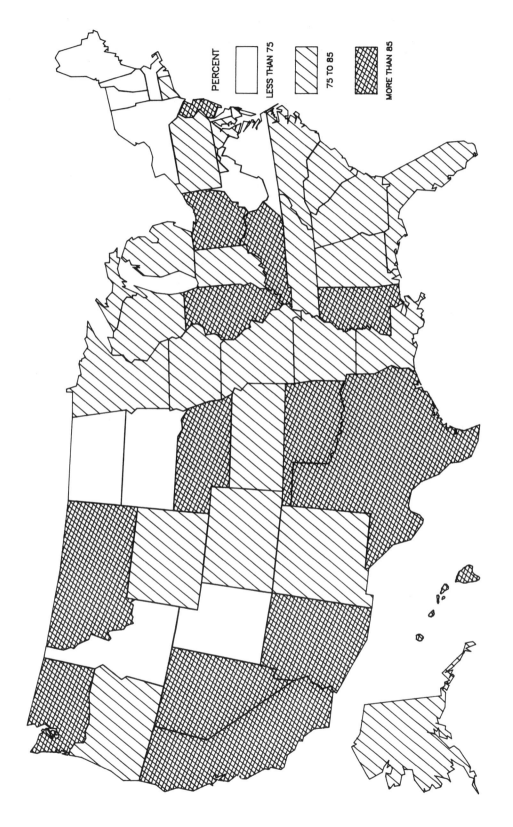

3.3 PROPORTION OF IN-STATE FRESHMEN, FALL 1988

PERCENT

LESS THAN 75

75 TO 85

MORE THAN 85

3.4 OUT-MIGRATION OF RECENT GRADUATES ENTERING FOUR-YEAR COLLEGES

This surface map shows, by state, the number of freshmen students entering four-year colleges who graduated from high school within the last twelve months and migrated out of their home states. The latest complete statistics available were for fall 1988. New Jersey lost the largest number of students, with out-migration of 20,671. New York was close behind with 20,130. Illinois lost the third largest number, 15,108, and Pennsylvania was fourth with 11,519. Four other states had more than 8,000 student out-migrants: Connecticut, Massachusetts, Maryland, and Ohio. All have large urban populations and are densely populated. Some of these states have both good state universities and excellent private institutions, so they would be expected to have a large in-migration of students as well.

At the other end of the spectrum, Utah had the smallest number of out-migrants. This probably reflects both the quality of Utah schools and the unique nature of Utah society, with its dominant Mormon culture. Other states with small numbers of out-migrants were chiefly small population states: Wyoming, North Dakota, Nevada, Idaho, Montana, South Dakota, and Alaska. All of them had fewer than 1,000 out-migrating students.

Nonetheless, it is apparent that this surface map does not simply mirror the distribution of population. California, the most populous state with almost 30 million people, lost fewer than 8,000 students, in comparison to the migration of over 20,000 from New Jersey, a state of slightly fewer than 8 million residents. The cost, quality, and reputation of both public and private schools are all factors in determining whether or not students stay in their home state to attend college. And, in addition, there are personal perceptions of the attractiveness and amenities of campuses. As in all migration models, the decision to go away to college is ultimately an individual one in which students weigh both push and pull factors.

The map shows that out-migration of students was concentrated in the eastern half of the country and to a considerable extent in the Northeast. In the South, only Florida and Georgia had outflows of more than 5,000. Western states did not generate nearly as many student migrants as eastern states. The discrepancy between size of population and size of the student migrant stream, already noted in California, was also apparent in Texas. Fewer than 6,000 students left their home state, with its population of about 17 million.

3.4 OUT-MIGRATION OF RECENT GRADUATES ENTERING FOUR-YEAR COLLEGES, FALL 1988

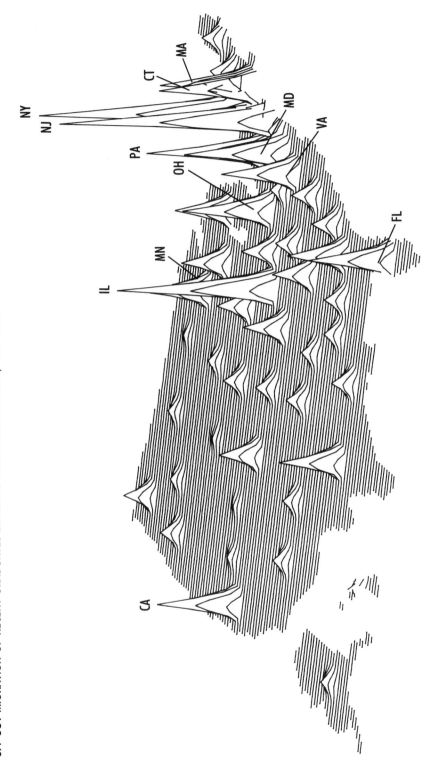

3.5 IN-MIGRATION OF RECENT GRADUATES ENTERING FOUR-YEAR COLLEGES

Overall, the map of in-migration of freshmen students by state looks surprisingly like the map of out-migration. The highest peaks are in the eastern half of the country. Massachusetts was the top destination for student migrants, with 16,457 out-of-state students entering the freshmen classes of the state in this year. Pennsylvania was second with 15,758, and New York third with 12,227. The densely populated urban states thus figured heavily in both in- and out-migration of students. Indiana (9,566) and Ohio (8,495) were also popular destinations. Again, size of state is a factor, as smaller eastern states have large numbers of out-migrating students, and the large western states have fewer.

There is a significant difference in this map, compared to the map of out-migration, when it comes to the South. There a number of states attracted large numbers of student migrants, perhaps because of climate and relatively low living costs. North Carolina, for example, had nearly 9,000 freshmen coming into its four-year colleges, while only a little over 2,000 left for other states. A similar situation existed in Alabama, which had over 5,000 in-migrants and lost fewer than 2,000. Georgia, however, was more like the urban states of the North, with its in- and out-migration almost exactly balanced at about 5,300. In the West, Colorado had the highest peak of in-migration at 5,131. California (4,998) and Texas (4,588) had significant in-migration, but not in proportion to their populations. Other peaks of in-migration in the West included Arizona (2,575), Oregon (2,578), and Washington (1,797).

3.5 IN-MIGRATION OF RECENT GRADUATES ENTERING FOUR-YEAR COLLEGES, FALL 1988

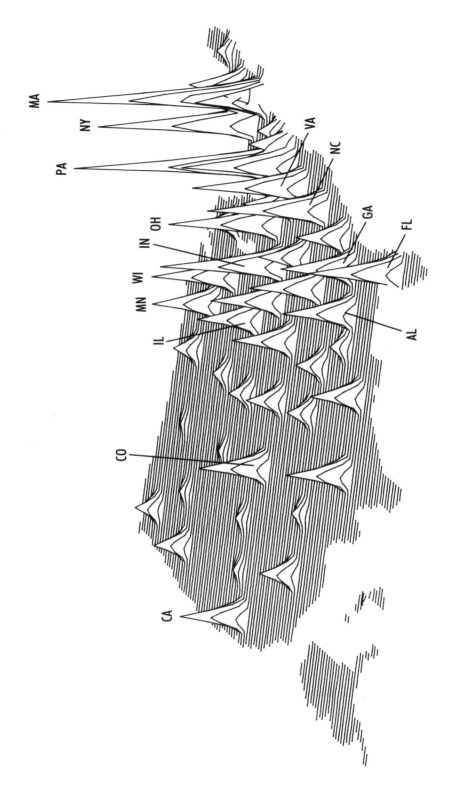

3.6 NET MIGRATION OF RECENT GRADUATES ENTERING FOUR-YEAR COLLEGES

This map is the sum of the previous two; it shows the migration of recent high school graduates who entered four-year colleges. Restricting the map to recent high school graduates ensures that it reflects college-bound freshmen of traditional age, rather than older students who return to school after migration to another state for employment or other reasons.

The basic premise behind the map is that students migrate to good colleges, not to poor ones, and therefore net migration is a kind of index of institutional quality. It may also be an index of institutional diversity, as some students also migrate out of state to enter particular programs.

The number of states with net in-migration and net out-migration are not evenly balanced; there are thirty states with net in-migration and twenty states with net out-migration. This imbalance is due in large part to the fact that only a few states "export" huge numbers of students while a much larger number "import" them. The surface map of out-migration shows that eight states each sent out more than 8,000 students: New Jersey, New York, Illinois, Pennsylvania, Connecticut, Massachusetts, Maryland, and Ohio. Many of their out-migrating students went to neighboring states; thus it is not surprising to find, for example, that the states contiguous to Illinois (which had a large net out-migration) all experienced net in-migration.

In many cases the amount of net migration was quite small, although significant numbers of students may have migrated in and out. California's net out-migration of slightly fewer than 3,000 students seems small in comparison to the large population of the state, the result of an out-migration of somewhat fewer than 8,000 students and an in-migration of about 5,000. The state of Georgia had a net in-migration of only 58, although both in- and out-migrants numbered over 5,000 each. While there is not a distinct regional pattern on this map, there is a relationship between it and the map showing the proportion of in-state residents. Those states with net out-migration (that is, those with limited in-migration) should have a larger proportion of in-state resident freshmen. In fact, this is the case, as twelve of the seventeen states with more than 80 percent of in-state residents are also states with net out-migration. Conversely, a comparison of the two maps should give some indication of the states that specialize in higher education—states with net in-migration and with a low proportion of in-state residents. Four such states stand out, all in New England: Vermont, New Hampshire, Massachusetts, and Rhode Island.

3.6 NET MIGRATION OF RECENT GRADUATES ENTERING FOUR-YEAR COLLEGES, FALL 1988

MIGRATION

OUT

IN

3.7 NUMBER OF FOREIGN STUDENTS BY STATE

Large numbers of foreign students study in American universities; in the 1990–91 school year they totaled nearly 390,000. The surface map shows that their distribution was far from even. California had by far the largest number of foreign students, over 55,000, followed by New York with more than 40,000. Third is Texas with over 26,000. Massachusetts had over 22,000 and Florida had almost 21,000. Illinois and Pennsylvania both had close to 18,000. Ohio had nearly 15,000 and Michigan over 14,000. No other state had more than 10,000 foreign students in this year, although New Jersey and the District of Columbia had just under that number. Six states with small populations had fewer than 1,000: Nevada, Vermont, South Dakota, Montana, Wyoming, and Alaska. Yet it seems rather more remarkable that South Dakota had nearly 800 foreign students and Wyoming had over 500 than that 55,000 found their way to the easily accessible, highly diverse, and generally low-cost opportunities for higher education in California. It appears that foreign students find their way to colleges in all states of the Union. It would also appear, in a first glance at the map, that their numbers correspond rather closely to the population size of the states. This is not entirely true, however. Although California and New York, the two largest states, had the largest populations of foreign students, Massachusetts had the third largest, and it is far from third largest in population. Massachusetts, with 6 million people in 1990, is slightly smaller than Georgia, North Carolina, and Virginia, all in the 6 million range. Yet it had three or four times as many foreign students as any of those three southern states.

3.7 NUMBER OF FOREIGN STUDENTS BY STATE, 1990

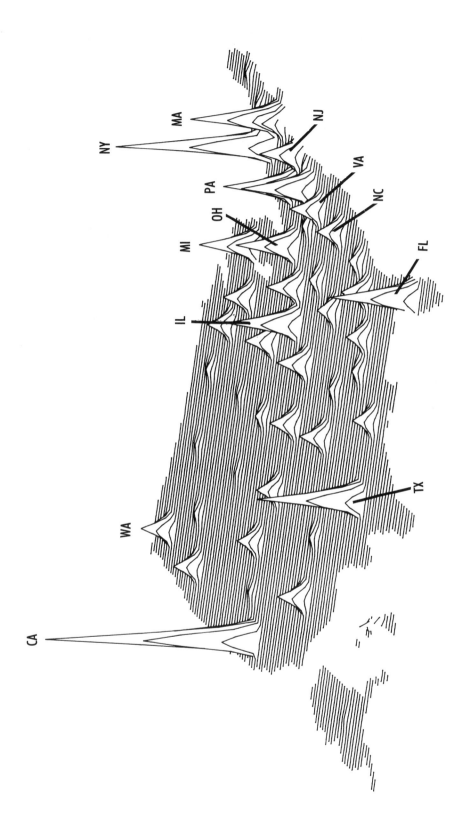

3.8 COLLEGES WITH THE LARGEST ENROLLMENT OF MERIT SCHOLARS

The map identifies the twenty-five colleges and universities that enrolled the largest numbers of Merit Scholars in 1991. In that year, over 6,500 freshmen Merit Scholars were enrolled throughout the country in nearly four hundred different institutions; 57 percent of them chose private schools, and 43 percent public ones, numbers that differed only slightly from the previous year. Not surprisingly, Merit Scholars tend to choose prestigious colleges, and the single largest contingent, 292 freshmen, chose Harvard/Radcliffe. However, an additional factor is whether or not institutions offer supplements to the scholarships, or whether students are solely funded by the National Merit Scholarship Corporation or other corporate sponsors.

Four Ivy League institutions are included among the top twenty-five. In addition to Harvard/Radcliffe's first rank, Yale was sixth with 144 scholars, Princeton seventh with 107, and Brown ranked nineteenth with 60. Four colleges in Texas—Rice University, University of Texas at Austin, Texas A. & M. University, and the University of Houston—were among the top twenty-five, as were three in California: Stanford University, University of California at Berkeley, and University of California at Los Angeles. All of the Texas institutions paid the cost of the scholarships for more than half of their Merit Scholars; the same was true of U.C.L.A. Stanford and Berkeley, however, did not sponsor additional scholarships.

Also prominent on the list are well-known institutes of technology—M.I.T., Georgia Tech, and Virginia Polytechnic Institute and State University.

Of the top twenty-five, the majority are private institutions. Among the state institutions, many of those attracting a large number of Merit Scholars provided additional support for a significant number of them, in most cases for around 70 to 80 percent. The only state institution that did not aid any of its fifty-eight scholars was the University of California at Berkeley.

In contrast, high-status private schools such as Harvard, Stanford, Yale, Princeton, M.I.T, Cornell, and Brown attracted Merit Scholars but did not provide additional funding. Duke funded only 10 of its 100 scholars. Other private schools did support quite a few of their Merit Scholars; for example, Carleton College sponsored 64 of its 86, Brigham Young 74 of 100, and Northwestern 71 of 105.

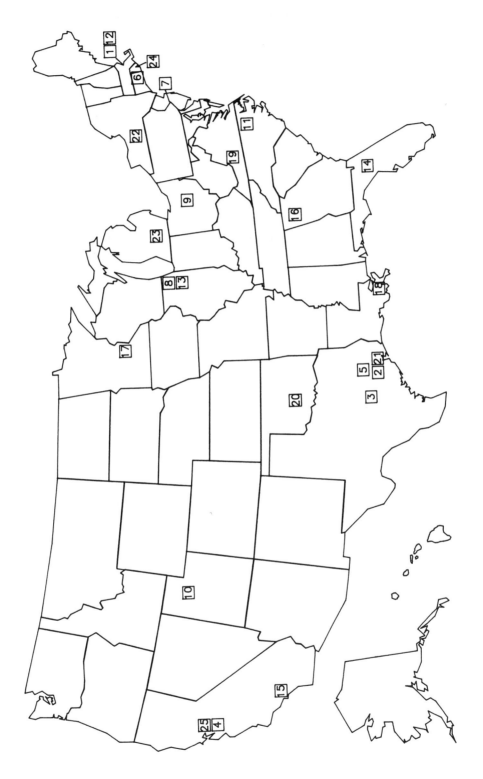

3.8 COLLEGES WITH THE LARGEST ENROLLMENT OF MERIT SCHOLARS, 1991

3.9 BACHELOR'S DEGREES CONFERRED IN BUSINESS

The map showing the proportion of bachelor's degrees granted in business is interesting and difficult to explain. The percentages in the legend are high, for business is a popular major throughout the United States. The state with the highest proportion of business degrees was Nevada, with over 38 percent; second was Mississippi, a very different kind of state in a different region, with 30 percent. Nevertheless, there is a discernible region in the South, including South Carolina, Georgia, Florida, Alabama, Mississippi, and Tennessee, as well as Missouri, Oklahoma, and Texas, in which business was a popular field of study. One might suggest that this is partially attributable to Sunbelt growth— a suggestion that is buttressed by the high percentage in Nevada, another Sunbelt state, and in Hawaii. But the other outliers with high proportions of business degrees were Vermont and Rhode Island in New England and New Jersey and Delaware in the Mid-Atlantic region, which are regions not experiencing considerable growth.

Business seems to be least popular as a field of study in the three West Coast states and in many states of the northern tier of the country. The state with the lowest percentage, slightly below 15 percent, was far northern and rural Maine.

3.9 BACHELOR'S DEGREES CONFERRED IN BUSINESS
(PROPORTION OF DEGREES CONFERRED, 1987)

PERCENT

LESS THAN 25.0

25.0 TO 28.0

MORE THAN 28.0

3.10 BACHELOR'S DEGREES CONFERRED IN EDUCATION

An interesting regionalization appears on this map. Education appears to be most popular as a degree option in states that are more rural, sparsely populated, and not very affluent. The most obvious clustering is a group of states in the northern Rockies and Great Plains area. It includes the Dakotas and Nebraska, Wyoming, Montana, Idaho, and Utah. Another grouping includes Oklahoma, Arkansas, and Mississippi. In the East, a single state in the high category is West Virginia, which has had a depressed economy and a declining population. Alaska, isolated, not very urbanized, and with a less developed higher education establishment, also falls into the high category.

The state with the highest percentage is Wyoming, with almost 27 percent of its baccalaureate degrees being granted in education. Arkansas, Oklahoma, and West Virginia are second, third, and fourth, respectively. A bloc of Atlantic Coast states from Maine to North Carolina form a major region with low proportions of students earning degrees in education. The lowest is the District of Columbia, with only 2.3 percent. However, California is second lowest with 2.6 percent, and several other states in the West (Washington, Arizona, and Colorado) also fall into the lowest category. Three midwestern states (Illinois, Michigan, and Indiana) and Florida are in this category as well.

3.10 BACHELOR'S DEGREES CONFERRED IN EDUCATION
(PROPORTION OF DEGREES CONFERRED, 1987)

PERCENT

LESS THAN 10.0

10.0 TO 15.0

MORE THAN 15.0

3.11 BACHELOR'S DEGREES CONFERRED IN AGRICULTURE

The highest proportions of degrees in agriculture are clearly concentrated in interior states, with a few surprising exceptions: Maine, Vermont, Delaware, and Alaska all fall into the high category, with more than 3 percent of bachelor's degrees granted in agriculture. Three percent may be a very small proportion, but so is the proportion of the American population that is engaged in agriculture.

The large "middle American" region with a relatively large proportion of degrees in agriculture extends from Wisconsin and Kentucky, which almost appear as eastern outliers, through a tier consisting of Iowa, Missouri, Arkansas, to a solid bloc extending from the Dakotas, Nebraska, and Kansas northwestward to Idaho. Many of these states are heavily dependent on agriculture and ranching, as well as sparsely populated and not very urbanized. The state with the largest proportion of degrees in agriculture is South Dakota, with 5.4 percent; it is followed in order by Montana, Wyoming, and North Dakota.

It may be that lack of incentive or opportunities to pursue degrees in a wide variety of fields contributes to this pattern, but certainly it also reflects the importance of agriculture and forestry in the economies of these states. They are largely neither heavily urban nor industrial. There is, however, a great difference between wealthy agricultural states, such as Wisconsin and Iowa, and poor states like Maine and Kentucky.

Regions in which agriculture degrees account for between 2 and 3 percent of all degrees granted are in the South and West. The urbanized northeastern quadrant of the country has the lowest percentages: for example, Massachusetts has 0.5 percent; Connecticut and New Jersey, 0.8; New York, 0.9 percent; and Rhode Island, 1.0 percent.

3.11 BACHELOR'S DEGREES CONFERRED IN AGRICULTURE
(PROPORTION OF DEGREES CONFERRED, 1987)

PERCENT

LESS THAN 2.0

2.0 TO 3.0

MORE THAN 3.0

3.12 BACHELOR'S DEGREES CONFERRED IN ENGINEERING

States in which a high percentage (more than 10%) of all baccalaureate degrees are in engineering are found in a strongly regionalized bloc. It extends from Montana and Wyoming eastward into the Dakotas and southward into the Four Corners states—Utah, Colorado, Arizona, and New Mexico. These states have many mining and irrigation projects that generate a heavy demand for engineers. Wyoming and New Mexico grant the highest proportion of such degrees, about 15 percent. Alaska also falls into the high category, which is appropriate for a frontier state with its many mining interests, particularly in North Slope oil. Louisiana is another state with major interests in oil and natural gas.

In the states east of the Mississippi, it is difficult to find explanations for the scattered states— Michigan and Indiana in the Midwest, Tennessee, Alabama, and Florida in the South, and Massachusetts in the Northeast. In the last case, M.I.T. may contribute heavily to this specialty in Massachusetts. States granting less than 8 percent of degrees in engineering are scattered. Arkansas, Vermont, New Hampshire, and Nebraska are at the bottom of the list, with less than 5 percent.

3.12 BACHELOR'S DEGREES CONFERRED IN ENGINEERING
(PROPORTION OF DEGREES CONFERRED, 1987)

PERCENT

LESS THAN 8.0

8.0 TO 10.0

MORE THAN 10.0

3.13 BACHELOR'S DEGREES CONFERRED IN THE SOCIAL SCIENCES

The highest percentages of social science degrees are concentrated in East Coast states, where twelve states in a belt extending from Maine to South Carolina conferred more than 10 percent of their degrees in the social sciences. The top value occurred in the District of Columbia, where over one-fifth (22%) of bachelor's degrees granted were in the social sciences. Vermont, Massachusetts, Connecticut, and Delaware ranked next. On the West Coast, California and Oregon both fell into the high category. In the interior of the country, Minnesota and South Dakota both were high, as were neighboring Utah and Colorado.

The states with high percentages tend to be states with many private liberal arts colleges, although Pennsylvania and Ohio, which also have many private liberal arts colleges, did not fall into the highest category.

On the other hand, the states with the lowest percentages of degrees in the social sciences are all interior or Gulf states. Many of them lack the dense population, large urban centers, and diversified ethnic groups that might be expected to generate interest and employment in the social sciences.

The lowest proportions of social science degrees granted are in Arkansas, North Dakota, Wyoming, Mississippi, West Virginia, and Nebraska, all with less than 5 percent.

3.13 BACHELOR'S DEGREES CONFERRED IN THE SOCIAL SCIENCES
(PROPORTION OF DEGREES CONFERRED, 1987)

PERCENT

LESS THAN 7.0

7.0 TO 10.0

MORE THAN 10.0

77

3.14 AVERAGE FACULTY SALARY

The first in this series of faculty-related maps focuses on faculty salary in the academic year 1989–90. This map is based on figures for full-time instructional faculty of all ranks on nine- or ten-month contracts at both public and private institutions. Nationally, the average salary for all ranks was $39,965. This figure masks wide variance among the ranks. Full professors that year earned an average of $52,809; associate professors, $39,381; assistant professors, $32,694; lecturers, $28,973; and instructors, $25,001.

The highest salaries, those above $40,000, were concentrated in two areas. The first and largest area was in the North, particularly in the states of the Megalopolis corridor from Massachusetts to Virginia. All of the southern New England and Mid-Atlantic states are included. Adjacent to this bloc were three Midwestern states: Ohio, Michigan, and Illinois. The second area of high salaries was in the West in California, Arizona, and Alaska. The two highest-paying states were at opposite ends of the country: Connecticut with an average faculty salary of $47,230, and California with $46,476. Massachusetts was a close third at $46,113.

For the most part, states in the intermediate-salary category, $35,000 to $40,000, tended to be located adjacent to the highest-salary states. The three states of northern New England were in this category, as were all the remaining midwestern states. Western states in this category included Washington and Hawaii on the Pacific, and a bloc including Nevada, Utah, and Colorado. Several southern states were in the intermediate category, notably Texas, Georgia, Florida, North Carolina, and Tennessee.

The remaining states were in the lowest average faculty salary category, less than $35,000. Most of these states are in a single broad region reaching from Oregon and Idaho in the Northwest, across the Rockies and the Plains to the states of the Deep South, excluding Georgia. New Mexico, Kentucky, and West Virginia were also in this lowest category. The three states with the lowest average faculty salaries were South Dakota, West Virginia, and Montana, all with averages between $29,400 and $29,800.

3.14 AVERAGE FACULTY SALARY
(ALL RANKS, FOUR-YEAR INSTITUTIONS, 1989–90)

DOLLARS

LESS THAN 35,000

35,000 TO 40,000

MORE THAN 40,000

3.15 AVERAGE FEMALE FACULTY SALARY AS A PERCENTAGE OF MALE SALARY

Like the map of average faculty salary, this map is based on average salary data at all public and private universities for faculty of all ranks on nine- or ten-month contracts. This map compares average female salary with average male salary. In 1989–90, in all fifty states and the District of Columbia, female faculty earned an average of $34,674. This was only 78 percent of the $44,041 earned by their male counterparts. This discrepancy largely reflects the relative concentration of women faculty in the lower academic ranks. In a rank-by-rank comparison, the differential between men and women, while still significant, is not as large. Female full professors, for example, earn 90 percent of the average earned by males; associate professors, 94 percent; assistant professors, 92 percent; and lecturers, 87 percent.

Regionally, the greatest differential, where women earn less then 79 percent as much as men, is in a bloc of six states in and near the Midwest from Iowa to Pennsylvania. The other states are concentrated in the South and include Virginia, Delaware, Tennessee, South Carolina, Texas, and Louisiana. Only two western states are in this category: Wyoming and Kansas. The states with the greatest sex differential in salaries are Wyoming, 74 percent; Delaware, 75 percent; and Indiana, 75 percent. In Wyoming the contrast is particularly marked at the lower ranks, although the small number of faculty in the state makes accurate generalization about individual ranks difficult.

States where women earn at least 81 percent as much as men, the highest category, are concentrated in the West. Alaska, Montana, Idaho, Oregon, Utah, New Mexico, and Oklahoma are all in this category. Only two states in this category, New Jersey and West Virginia, lie outside the West. The greatest degree of parity is achieved in Alaska, where women faculty earn 92 percent as much as men faculty. In fact, in one category, full professor, women earned $56,414—a few hundred dollars more than their male colleagues. No other state comes close to Alaska's figure, however. The next closest in equality of pay are Idaho and Montana, both at 85 percent differential. A comparison with the previous map shows that states with smaller differentials in salary between male and female faculty tend to be states in the lowest average salary category: West Virginia, Oklahoma, New Mexico, Montana, Idaho, and Oregon. This statement is thus true for six of the nine states with the lowest differential. On the other hand, two states with the lowest differential between men and women, New Jersey and Alaska, are among the highest faculty salary states.

States in the intermediate group, where female faculty salaries are between 79 percent and 81 percent that of male faculty, are concentrated in New York and all of New England; in a band of southern states from Arkansas through the Deep South to North Carolina (except South Carolina); in the northern Midwest and northern Great Plains states; and in California and the southwestern states of Arizona and Nevada.

3.15 AVERAGE FEMALE FACULTY SALARY AS A PERCENTAGE OF MALE SALARY
(ALL RANKS, 1989–90)

PERCENT

LESS THAN 79

79 TO 81

MORE THAN 81

3.16 STUDENT-FACULTY RATIO

This map shows the ratio of students (total FTE enrollment) to full-time instructional staff in fall 1989. States with relatively high ratios of students to faculty are concentrated in three areas: the Northeast, including three of the New England states as well as New York, Pennsylvania, and New Jersey; the Great Plains, including Texas, Kansas, and Nebraska; and the West, in California, Nevada, and Arizona. The states with the lowest student-faculty ratios, those below 12.5, are quite scattered. Wyoming has the lowest ratio—6.7 students per faculty.

States in the intermediate category, where the ratio of students to faculty is from 12.5 to 15, are found in all parts of the country, with concentrations in the Midwest and northern Great Plains states. States with the lowest student-faculty ratios, less than 12.5 to 1, are located in the more rural parts of the nation the South, the Northwest, and the states of the central Rockies (Wyoming, Colorado, and Utah).

To an extent, the pattern appears to reflect the principle of economy of scale. Most of the ten most populated states are in the category with the highest ratios. Most of the states with small populations, including Wyoming, Delaware, Vermont, and Rhode Island, are in the category with the lowest ratios. There are exceptions, however, as Maine, a state with a small population, has the highest student-faculty ratio (24 to 1), while North Carolina, one of the ten largest states, has the third lowest ratio (about 10 to 1).

3.16 STUDENT-FACULTY RATIO
(FTE STUDENTS AND FTE INSTRUCTIONAL STAFF, 1989)

RATIO

☐ LESS THAN 12.5

▨ 12.5 TO 15.0

▨ MORE THAN 15.0

4

Cultural Diversity

4.1 PERCENTAGE OF MINORITIES IN HIGHER EDUCATION

Cultural diversity and minority enrollment in higher education are topics of great interest for the 1990s, given demographic projections that show increasing numbers and percentages of minority children entering the school system. Eight maps have been devoted to the subject, showing first the overall pattern of minority enrollment in higher education, then taking each minority group—black Americans, Hispanics, Asians, and Native Americans—and presenting maps that explain or elucidate the overall pattern. Minority groups have distinctive patterns of distribution in the overall population, as shown in the background maps in chapter 1. African-Americans are concentrated in the Southeast and in many large cities in other parts of the country, especially in the Northeast, Midwest, and California. Hispanics are concentrated in the Southwest from California to Texas, in southern Florida, and in New York. The location of the Native American population is directly tied to the pattern of Indian reservations. The Asian population, now rapidly growing in many areas, is still concentrated in the West, particularly in Hawaii and California, but is also well represented in metropolitan areas in the East. The first map shows the percentage of minority enrollment by state in 1990. This map includes all four ethnic groups, and a remarkable pattern emerges. The highest category of minority enrollment forms almost a complete rim, or peripheral pattern, around the eastern, southern, and western limits of the country. States with high percentages include New York and New Jersey and, with only small Delaware excluded, continue down along the East Coast, all of the southern states, and then continue from Texas to California. Alaska and Hawaii are also included in this periphery of high values. In the interior of the country, only Illinois, with multi-ethnic Chicago, is in the high category. The map is explained by the distribution of all the groups in the general population. Clearly the distribution of African-Americans heavily influences the distribution pattern, as all southern and border states have percentages over 15. The distribution of Hispanics reinforces this pattern in the big-city states and in California and the Southwest. The influence of the relatively small numbers of Asians and Native Americans on this overall map of minority distribution is less marked, although the large enrollment of Asians in California is a contributing factor to its large minority percentage. The figures from which the map was constructed give more insights into the distribution patterns. Three states have more than 30 percent minority enrollment Hawaii (63.2%), New Mexico (36.8%), and California (32.4%). The District of Columbia, too small to appear on the map, also has a 36 percent minority enrollment. The Pacific Island state of Hawaii is unique; the word "minority" has little meaning there, and there are twice as many Asian students as white. New Mexico and California are the two mainland states in which about one in three college students is a member of a minority group. New Mexico's very large minority population is predominantly Hispanic and Native American. California's is about equally accounted for by Hispanics and Asians. California, as the state with the largest population, is home to many members of all minority groups. Thus it in fact has the largest absolute numbers of both black and Native American students of any state, but the percentages for these groups are small. At the other end of the scale, the map shows areas where low percentages of minority students are enrolled. Northern New England is one such region, and West Virginia stands out as an isolated state with a low percentage of minority enrollment. The other states in the low category are in the northern interior area of the country.

4.1 PERCENTAGE OF MINORITIES IN HIGHER EDUCATION, 1990

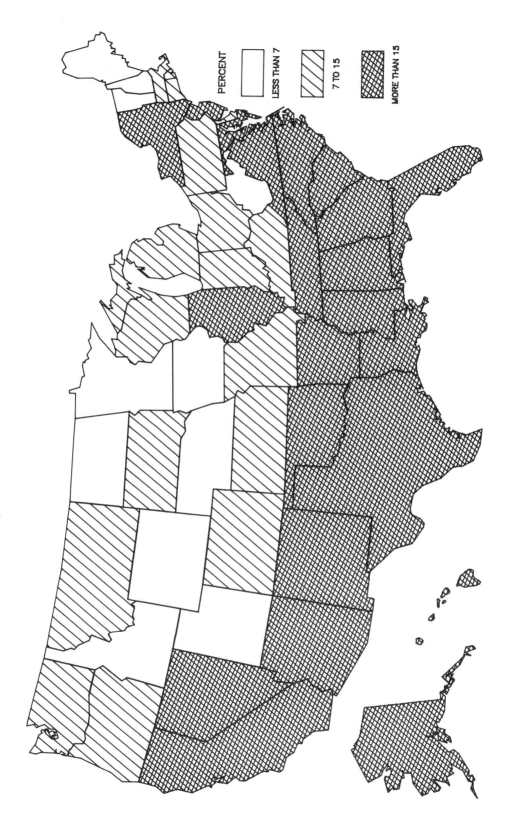

PERCENT

LESS THAN 7

7 TO 15

MORE THAN 15

4.2 AFRICAN-AMERICANS IN HIGHER EDUCATION

This map shows African-American students as a percentage of total students enrolled, by state. It can be easily compared with the previous map showing total minority enrollment percentages; it is clear that the distribution of black students is a major component in the overall minority map. It is also clear that the highest percentages of black students are found in the Southeast; the proportions of blacks in higher education are strongly influenced by their percentages in the total population. The southeastern bloc of states from Maryland and Delaware to Louisiana and Arkansas, where more than 15 percent of the overall population is black, have more than 10 percent black enrollment. New York, New Jersey, and Illinois, northern states with large-city black populations, also fall into the high category. In the middle category, with 3.5 to 10 percent African-American enrollment, are all other states east of the Mississippi, except the three northern New England states. West of the Mississippi, Missouri, Kansas, Oklahoma, and Texas fall into this category, as do California, Nevada, and Alaska. A large bloc of interior states, as well as Washington, Oregon, and Hawaii, have less than 3.5 percent African-American enrollment. They are states in which the overall proportion of blacks in the population is also low.

The proportion of African-Americans in higher education enrollment is in most cases less than their proportion in the total population. The most dramatic case is the District of Columbia, where 65.8 percent of the population is African-American, but only 30.7 percent of the college enrollment. Students migrate in to the many universities in the District, although a small number of institutions, such as the University of the District of Columbia, draw predominantly on local students. In Mississippi, African-Americans make up 35.6 percent of the total population, but 27.4 percent of enrollment. South Carolina, Georgia, and Louisiana have similar disparities. In contrast, some of the states with very small African-American populations, such as Maine, Idaho, and Vermont, have higher percentages of this minority group enrolled in higher education than the percentage in the total population.

4.2 AFRICAN-AMERICANS IN HIGHER EDUCATION
(PERCENTAGE OF TOTAL ENROLLMENT, 1990)

PERCENT

LESS THAN 3.5

3.5 TO 10

MORE THAN 10

4.3 PREDOMINANTLY BLACK INSTITUTIONS

Another aspect of the geography of African-Americans in higher education is the map of predominantly black colleges and universities. Again, the pattern reflects the distribution of the African-American population, but it reflects that pattern at an earlier date. Most of the institutions that are shown on the map were founded in the period from the Civil War to World War I, a time when educational segregation denied black students access to the established college systems in the South or in other white private colleges. The map includes all those colleges that belong to the National Association for Equal Opportunity in Higher Education (NAFEO), an organization founded in 1969 by historically black institutions. Some 117 "historically and traditionally black colleges and universities" belong to NAFEO. They include public and private, two-year and four-year colleges, plus black graduate and professional schools. The institutions enroll between a quarter and a half million students. Also included on the map are eleven other institutions listed by NAFEO as equal opportunity colleges and universities that are predominantly black.

While most of these institutions are located in a belt of southern and border states extending from Maryland and Delaware to Texas, some of the oldest are in Pennsylvania and Ohio, some of them founded even before the Civil War. There are also newer predominantly black schools in Massachusetts, New York, Michigan, and California.

Notable on the map is Atlanta, long a bastion of black education. It is the home of five traditionally black institutions: Morehouse College and Morehouse School of Medicine (shown together by one dot), Spelman College, Atlanta University, Clark College, and Morris Brown College, plus the more recently founded Atlanta Metropolitan College.

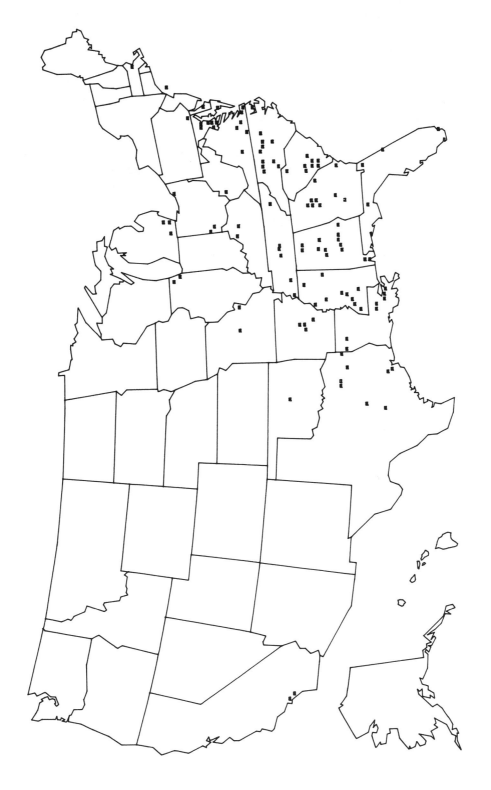

4.4 HISPANICS IN HIGHER EDUCATION

The pattern of Hispanic enrollment in higher education is strongly regionalized and, given current demographic trends, is apt to become more so. There have been dramatic increases in the Hispanic population, largely due to international migration, though also to natural increase. The numbers of young people generated by the rapid increase in Hispanic population will continue to fuel increases in college enrollment. The largest percentages of Hispanic enrollment are found in the areas one would expect after examining the Hispanic population distribution map. There is a belt of states extending from California to Texas, with a northward extension into Colorado. New Mexico ranks first: nearly 28 percent of its enrolled students are Hispanic. Texas is second with 16.5 percent, California third with 12.6 percent, and Arizona fourth with 11.2 percent. Florida is also in the high category, ranking fifth with 10.9 percent. The big urban populations of New York, New Jersey, and Illinois put them into the highest category as well. Other urban states in the industrial Northeast fall into the middle category, with one to five percent Hispanic enrollment. So do the states adjacent to the heavily Hispanic Southwest region. There is a very low proportion of Hispanic enrollment, less than one percent, in many southern states, in two New England states, and in a bloc of northern interior states.

4.4 HISPANICS IN HIGHER EDUCATION
(PERCENTAGE OF TOTAL ENROLLMENT, 1990)

PERCENT

LESS THAN 1

1 TO 5

MORE THAN 5

4.5 HISPANIC-SERVING INSTITUTIONS

A second map on Hispanics shows the distribution of colleges classified as Hispanic-serving institutions in the directory of the Hispanic Association of Colleges and Universities. In all of these institutions at least 25 percent of enrolled students are Hispanic. In some of them the percentage is very high, as at Laredo Junior College in Texas (90%) or Hostos Community College in the Bronx (over 80%). Although the Hispanic-serving institutions run the gamut from large four-year state and private universities to very small Catholic seminaries, they are predominantly two-year, publicly supported colleges. About two-thirds of the colleges fall into the community college category, and some of them are quite large. The huge Miami-Dade Community College in Florida, with a total enrollment of about 44,000, is over 50 percent Hispanic. The map clearly shows that the colleges that serve Hispanics are found in the same states that have large Hispanic populations; they are largely two-year public institutions. They vary considerably, due to the diverse nationalities grouped as "Hispanic." Students in the West are chiefly of Mexican origin; those in southern Florida are mostly Cuban and Central American, and those at institutions in New York City are likely to be Puerto Rican.

4.5 HISPANIC-SERVING INSTITUTIONS, 1990

△ 25–50% HISPANIC
□ MORE THAN 50% HISPANIC

4.6 ASIANS IN HIGHER EDUCATION

Much has been written about Asians in higher education in the United States because of their reputation for high academic achievement and because their number is increasing rapidly through international migration. Although their percentage in the total U.S. population is small, they form large minorities in certain metropolitan areas. Regional patterns are not as easy to describe as those of the other three minority groups. Although concentrated in Hawaii and the Pacific states, Asians have spread throughout the country, chiefly in the larger urban areas. A major problem is the all-inclusiveness of the term "Asian"; it is a geographical term referring to the place of origin of many different national and ethnic groups. In the census, the category "Asians and Pacific Islanders" includes Chinese, Japanese, Vietnamese, Korean, Filipino, Pakistani, Indian, and many others. Each of these groups has its own pattern of distribution within the United States; some patterns are long established and others quite recent. For example, the Vietnamese population is largely of post-1975 origin, but the Chinese communities along the West Coast date back to the 1800s.

In terms of overall population distribution, Asians are highly concentrated in Hawaii and on the West Coast. Hawaii is really in a class by itself, as some two-thirds of its population is Asian, including Japanese, Filipinos, and many other nationalities. On the mainland, Asians have long formed the largest minorities in the West, especially in the Pacific states. They are highly concentrated in large metropolitan areas; by 1985 Los Angeles had become the first American city to have an Asian population of more than one million. Four cities—Los Angeles, San Francisco, Honolulu, and New York—accounted for an additional three million. No other city had more than 250,000 Asians, but most did have some Asian minorities. In the less urbanized states, the Asian minority almost disappears.

In terms of percentages of Asians in higher education, Hawaii ranks first with 58.3 percent, followed by California with 12.2 percent, and Washington with 5.9 percent. No other state had as much as 5 percent. Because overall percentages are so low, the high category on the map includes states with over 3 percent. They are Hawaii, the West Coast states, Nevada, Texas, Illinois, and a group of states in the highly urbanized East Coast region. These include New York (ranked fourth with 4.7%), Massachusetts, New Jersey, Maryland, and Virginia. The fact that so many states fall into the middle category of one to three percent shows the widespread distribution but low percentages of Asians. States in which less than one percent of higher education enrollment is Asian include Maine, some southern states, and a bloc of four in the northern Plains and Rocky Mountain states —North and South Dakota, Wyoming, and Montana.

4.6 ASIANS IN HIGHER EDUCATION
(PERCENTAGE OF TOTAL ENROLLMENT, 1990)

PERCENT

LESS THAN 1

1 TO 3

MORE THAN 3

4.7 NATIVE AMERICANS IN HIGHER EDUCATION

The simplest spatial pattern among American minorities is that of the Native Americans, including American Indians and Inuit. This minority is the smallest in number and is also the most place-bound. The Inuit are still located in their homeland in Alaska. Most American Indians still live on reservations or in their vicinity, except in Oklahoma. The descendants of the survivors of the eastern tribes who were resettled in Oklahoma live there today, intermixed with the general population. The remaining western tribes live chiefly in the Southwest, principally in Arizona and New Mexico, and in the northern Great Plains and Rocky Mountain states. Native Americans total only about 1,959,000 in the whole U.S. population. Oklahoma, California, Arizona, and New Mexico are the only states in which there are over 100,000 Native Americans. In terms of percentages of college enrollment, the numbers are very small. The high is 8.9 percent in Alaska, and Montana ranks second with 6.8 percent. South Dakota, Oklahoma, and New Mexico come next, all with more than 5 percent. All of the states in the middle category, with between one and five percent Native American enrollment in higher education, are in the western half of the country. No state east of the Dakotas or Oklahoma has as much as one percent.

4.7 NATIVE AMERICANS IN HIGHER EDUCATION
(PERCENTAGE OF TOTAL ENROLLMENT, 1990)

PERCENT

LESS THAN 1

1 TO 5

MORE THAN 5

4.8 NATIVE AMERICAN COLLEGES

Although many Native American students are enrolled in the public systems or in church-supported private colleges, some attention has been attracted to a recent phenomenon, the Indian-controlled "tribal" colleges. The first one was established in Arizona in 1968, and the first comprehensive study of them was published by the Carnegie Foundation for the Advancement of Teaching in 1989. There are now twenty-seven of these small colleges, most of them on tribal reservations. Although they are small and poorly funded, they are active and have formed an American Indian Higher Education Consortium. They enroll a total of perhaps 5,000 full-time students, with other students enrolled part-time.

All are two-year colleges offering associate degrees, except for two four-year colleges in South Dakota. One of them, Sinte Gleska College in Rosebud, renamed itself Sinte Gleska University in 1992. The map shows that they are concentrated in Montana and the Dakotas. These institutions, almost all in rural locations, provide access to higher education for people for whom a college education would otherwise be impossible. In addition to offering vocational and general education programs, the colleges seek to preserve Indian languages and culture.

4.8 NATIVE AMERICAN COLLEGES, 1992

5

Specialized Institutions

5.1 ABA-APPROVED LAW SCHOOLS

The United States has a higher ratio of lawyers to population than any other country in the world, about one lawyer per three hundred people, as recently reported by the American Bar Association. The training of these lawyers is an important aspect of higher education. In 1990, more than 94,000 students applied to law schools. Competition for places in the best schools is keen; the law is a prestigious, remunerative, and powerful profession. More than half the members of Congress are lawyers.

The accompanying map shows the distribution of the schools that were approved by the American Bar Association in 1990. It includes 178 law schools that are members of the Association of American Law Schools, plus sixteen others that are also approved by the ABA. Only two states, Alaska and Nevada, have no approved law schools. It is clear that when there are so many schools, they must roughly reflect the distribution of the population, with a heavier pattern in the eastern part of the country. There are notable clusters in Megalopolis, the urbanized region extending from Boston to Washington; in the Chicago area; and in the two large conurbations of California, the San Francisco Bay Area and the Los Angeles–San Diego area. Most states operate at least one law school in the state university, often at the flagship university. States with larger populations have several state-supported law schools. California, the largest state in population, has five state-supported law schools. In addition, California has ten private schools. California's pattern is representative of the whole country: there are many private law schools, ranging from small, independent schools to the famous schools of law incorporated in distinguished private universities such as Harvard, Yale, Stanford, and Chicago.

5.1 ABA-APPROVED LAW SCHOOLS, 1991

5.2 ACCREDITED MEDICAL SCHOOLS

The map shows the distribution of accredited medical schools, based on data provided by the Association of American Medical Colleges. Like the law schools, there is a clear association with population, resulting in a higher density of medical schools in the eastern part of the country. There are fewer U.S. medical schools than law schools, however: only 124. For example, California has nine medical schools, compared to sixteen law schools, and the nine are concentrated in the conurbations around San Francisco Bay and in the Los Angeles–San Diego area. It is apparent that medical schools exhibit a strong affinity for urban areas, where large teaching hospitals are available. New York has twelve medical schools, the largest number of any state, and seven of them are in the New York City metropolitan area. Five of Pennsylvania's seven medical schools are in Philadelphia, and six of the seven medical colleges in Illinois are in Chicago. Other metropolitan areas with multiple medical colleges are Boston and Washington, D.C., with three; and Baltimore, New Orleans, Atlanta, Nashville, Houston, and Omaha with two. The association of medical schools with population distribution can be seen in the fact that the ten largest states in terms of population (California, New York, Texas, Florida, Pennsylvania, Illinois, Ohio, Michigan, New Jersey, and North Carolina), which together have about half of the nation's people, contain almost half of the medical schools. Most states have at least one medical school, even small states such as Rhode Island, Delaware, New Hampshire, and Vermont. Only four states have no medical schools. They are Maine and three sparsely populated states in the northern Rocky Mountains area—Idaho, Montana, and Wyoming.

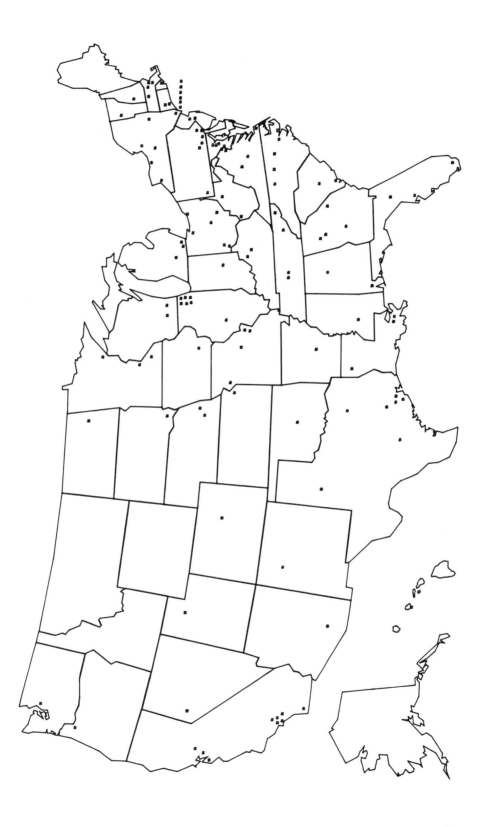

5.2 ACCREDITED MEDICAL SCHOOLS, 1991

5.3 ACCREDITED COLLEGES OF VETERINARY MEDICINE

In contrast to the large number of medical schools and even larger numbers of law schools in the country, there are only twenty-seven veterinary medical schools, enrolling a total of about 8,500 students. As shown on the map, the distribution of veterinary medical schools is heaviest in the more populated eastern half of the country. It is also related to the pattern of agricultural areas. In addition to caring for the pets of urban dwellers, veterinarians are essential in agricultural areas with large numbers of farm animals. Thus many veterinary schools are located at land-grant colleges. Relatively few private institutions, therefore, have schools of veterinary medicine. These exceptions include Tufts, the University of Pennsylvania, Tuskegee Institute, and Cornell University. Cornell, although a private university, operates several units of the State University of New York, including the veterinary school. Only one state, Alabama, has more than one school of veterinary medicine, with schools at Auburn University and Tuskegee Institute. The Tuskegee School of Veterinary Medicine is the only predominantly black veterinary medical institution in the country, and it draws students from more states than does any other institution, including states as far away as California and New Jersey. Not every state has a veterinary medical college. Those that do not have made arrangements with a school in another state to reserve spaces. For example, the University of Georgia serves South Carolina, Kansas serves Nebraska, and the University of Pennsylvania serves New Jersey. In some cases, the pairing arrangement would not be immediately apparent from the map. Auburn University in Alabama has an arrangement to serve Kentucky students, and the University of Missouri serves Nevada.

There are only four veterinary schools west of the Great Plains. Colorado's veterinary medical school at Colorado State in Fort Collins is the most striking example of a single, centrally located school serving a large, relatively sparsely populated region. It is also one of the largest veterinary medical school in terms of enrollment. Its role is analogous to that of the dental school at the University of Colorado in Denver. In addition to Colorado itself, its students come from Arizona, Montana, New Mexico, Utah, and Wyoming. The College of Veterinary Medicine in Pullman, Washington, as its location in the eastern part of the state suggests, serves students from neighboring Idaho. Oregon maintains its own school, which has the smallest enrollment of any veterinary training institution in the country. California's only school, at the University of California at Davis, is quite large; it draws its enrollment primarily from the state of California itself. California students, however, also go to schools in many other states.

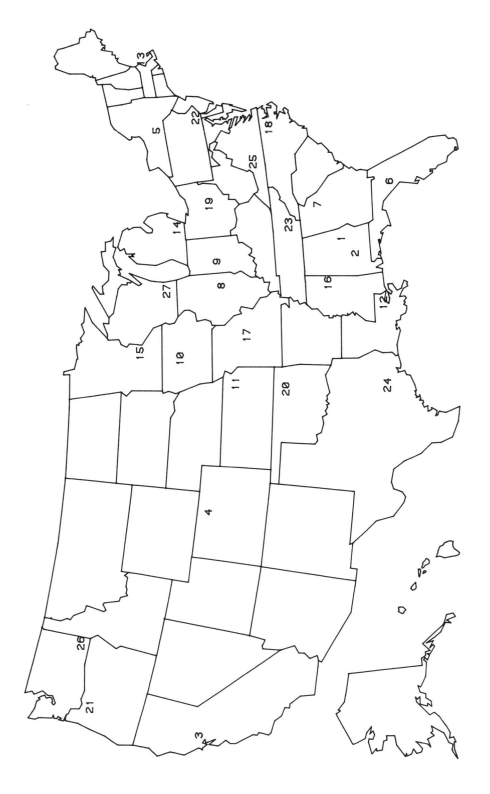

5.4 ACCREDITED DENTAL SCHOOLS

Schools of dentistry display about the same distribution pattern as do medical schools; that is, the pattern follows the distribution of population, with a strong affinity for urban areas. There were, however, only thirty-nine fully operational dental schools in 1991, compared to about 130 medical schools. Three universities (Emory University in Atlanta, Georgetown University in D.C., and Oral Roberts University in Tulsa) are in the process of closing down their dental schools. Only states with large populations have more than one dental school. California is first with five, New York and Illinois have four, and Massachusetts, Pennsylvania, and Texas each have three. Large regions are without dental schools; there is only one, at the University of Colorado, in the whole Rocky Mountain region. And in the tier of Great Plains states stretching north of Texas, there are only three—two in Nebraska (both in Omaha) and one in Oklahoma.

Almost all schools of dentistry are co-located with schools of medicine. For example, there is the University of Medicine and Dentistry of New Jersey at Newark. The dental school for the University of Georgia system is in Augusta at the Medical College of Georgia, and the South Carolina dental school is at the Medical University of South Carolina in Charleston. The pairing rule holds at many private universities—Harvard, Tufts, Boston, Howard, and Northwestern, to name just a few, have both medical and dental schools. Three exceptions, all at private universities, are the dental schools at Marquette University in Wisconsin, at the University of the Pacific in California, and at Fairleigh Dickinson University in New Jersey. There are many states without dental schools, notably in northern New England and in the small states of Rhode Island and Delaware, as well as Arkansas; most outstanding, however, is a bloc of states stretching west from the Dakotas to Idaho and south to New Mexico. The presence of a dental school, along with a medical school, at the University of Colorado in Denver underscores the importance of that city as a regional educational center for this large area.

5.4 ACCREDITED DENTAL SCHOOLS, 1991

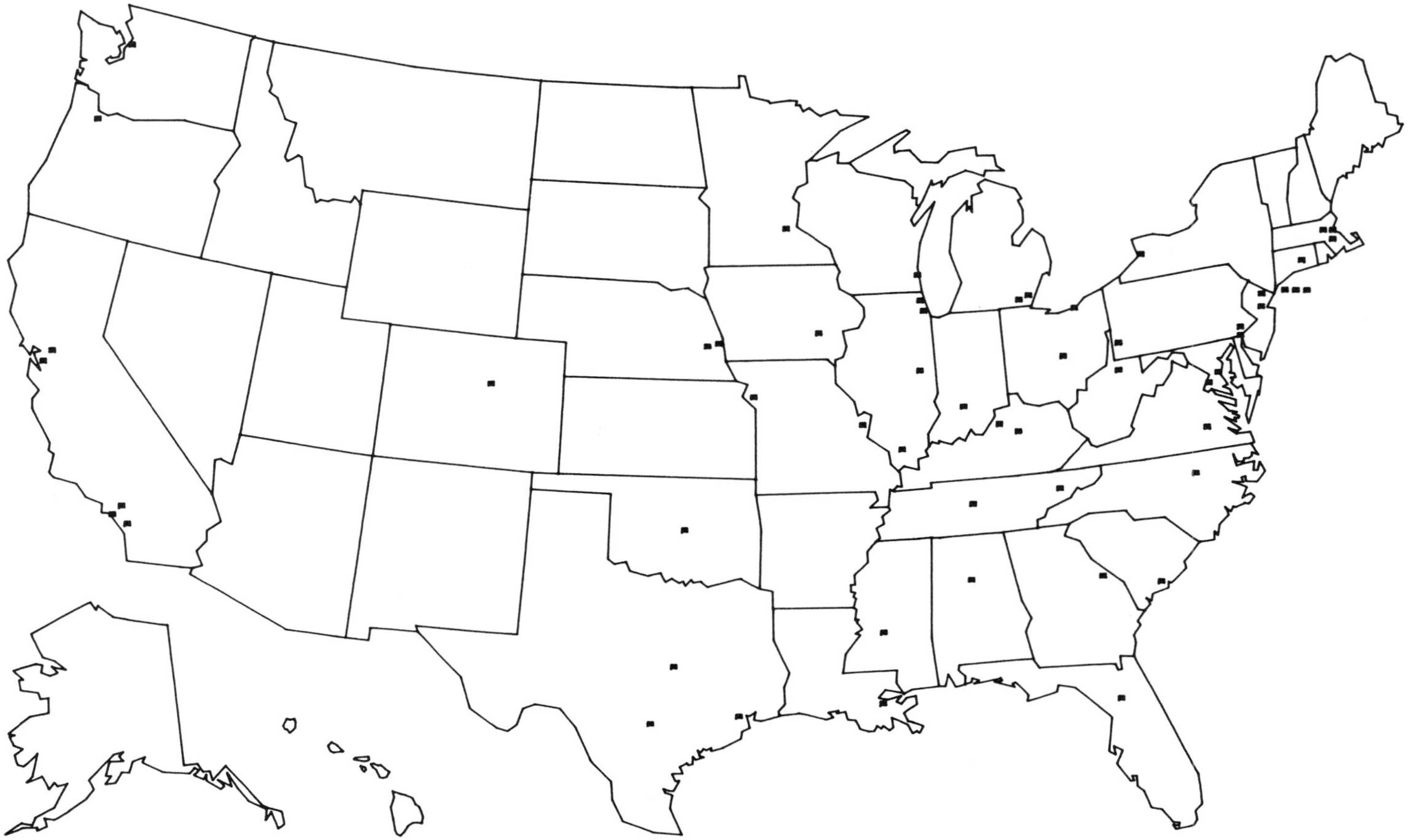

5.5 INSTITUTIONS GRANTING THE LARGEST NUMBER OF DOCTORAL DEGREES

The map showing the twenty-five institutions that granted the largest numbers of doctoral degrees in the ten-year period from academic year 1978–79 through 1987–88 is a highly regionalized map. Nineteen of the institutions are located in the northeastern quadrant of the United States. Five are on the West Coast: four in California and one in Washington. Only one institution outside these two regions makes the list, the University of Texas at Austin.

Each of these institutions granted a total of well over 3,000 doctoral degrees in the ten-year period. Degrees included are the Ph.D., Ed.D., and comparable degrees at the doctoral level; first professional degrees such as M.D., D.D.S., and D.V.M. are not included.

The four top doctoral granting institutions are all public—the flagship institutions of four populous states, all with excellent state systems. They are the University of California, Berkeley; University of Wisconsin, Madison; University of Michigan, Ann Arbor; and University of Illinois, Urbana. Each granted close to or in excess of 6,000 doctoral degrees in the ten-year period. The fifth is a private university, Columbia, also with almost 6,000 doctoral graduates.

In all, fifteen of these twenty-five institutions granting the largest number of doctoral degrees are state universities and ten are private ones.

5.5 INSTITUTIONS GRANTING THE LARGEST NUMBER OF DOCTORAL DEGREES, 1979–88

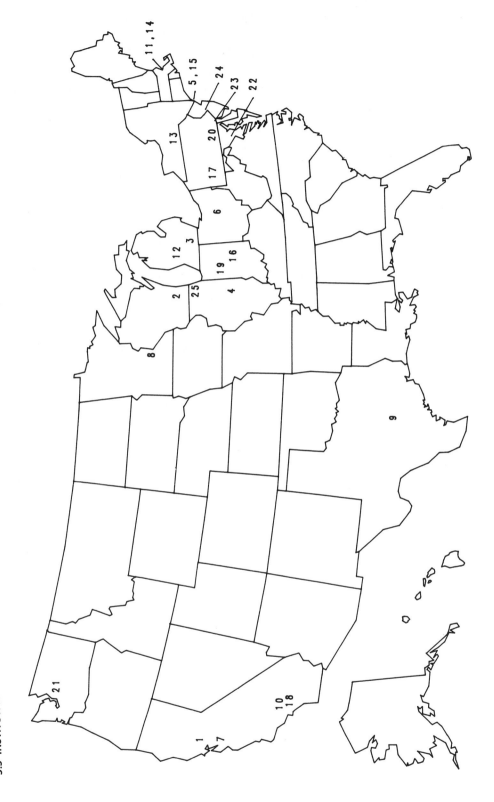

5.6 FIFTY LARGEST UNIVERSITY RESEARCH LIBRARIES

The map shows the fifty largest university research libraries in the United States in 1990, ranked by number of volumes. Not surprisingly, this map shows a close correspondence with the map on which leading research universities, as ranked by the Carnegie Foundation in 1987, have been located. What is perhaps more surprising is the fact that the maps do not correspond even more closely. Some universities with large research libraries did not make the list of leading research universities (for example, Arizona State, the University of Oklahoma, and SUNY-Buffalo). Conversely, some of the institutions that made the Carnegie list as leading research universities are not among the fifty with the largest libraries (e.g., one in Texas, one in Colorado, one in Utah, one in Miami, etc.).

All the universities with large libraries can, however, be designated as prestigious, research-oriented institutions. Of the fifty, thirty-four are public institutions and sixteen are private, but five of the top ten are private. Harvard comes first, with nearly twelve million volumes, followed by Yale with nearly nine million. The next five are big state institutions—the University of Illinois, the University of California at Berkeley, the University of Michigan, the University of Texas, and U.C.L.A.—all in the six or seven million range. Then come four more prestigious private universities—Columbia, Stanford, Cornell, and Chicago.

These large research libraries are concentrated in urban areas of the East Coast states and in the Midwest, with secondary clusters in the two big urban areas of California. In northern New England, the interior states of the South, and in the Great Plains and Rocky Mountain states, there are very few large research libraries.

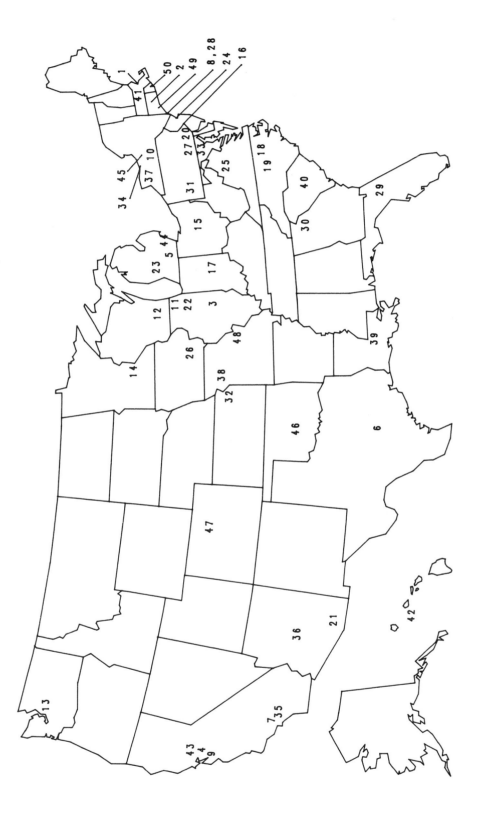

5.6 FIFTY LARGEST UNIVERSITY RESEARCH LIBRARIES, 1990

5.7 LEADING RESEARCH UNIVERSITIES, PUBLIC AND PRIVATE

This map shows the location of seventy universities that the Carnegie Foundation classified as leading research universities in 1987. These universities emphasize graduate study through the doctoral degree and give a high priority to research. Most of them have a full range of baccalaureate programs, each of them awards at least fifty Ph.D. degrees per year, and each receives at least $33.5 million annually in federal support.

The distribution of these leading research universities is not at all even. Many states have none, while certain urban areas have a heavy concentration. New York City leads with four; there are three each in the Boston, Chicago, Los Angeles, and San Francisco areas.

The overall pattern is one of concentration in the East, particularly in the northeast quadrant of the country, and even more specifically in the highly urbanized Megalopolis stretching from Boston to Washington, D.C., where a total of fifteen public and private major research universities are located. In the Southeast, North Carolina has three, and two each are found in Georgia, Florida, and Virginia. There are, however, none in South Carolina, Alabama, or Mississippi.

There is also a large region in the middle of the country that does not contain any of these premier research institutions. It stretches north and west from Arkansas and Oklahoma through the Great Plains to the mountains of Montana, Idaho, and Wyoming. To the south and west of this region, the Four Corners states of Colorado, New Mexico, Arizona, and Utah fare better, however. The West Coast states have a total of eleven of the leading research universities, one each in Washington and Oregon and nine in California. It is hardly surprising that California has the largest total, in view of its population size. While it is not surprising that the California institutions are found in two nodes, the Bay Area and the Los Angeles–San Diego corridor, it is rather remarkable that nine of the eleven are public institutions. This is in contrast to New York, where six of the seven premier institutions are private. Of the seventy universities that meet the Carnegie criteria, forty-five are public and twenty-five are private. All but four of the private institutions are east of the Mississippi River. One of these four, Washington University in Saint Louis, is barely across the river, so that in reality the only three private research universities in the West are in California—two in Los Angeles and one in the Bay Area. Furthermore, the private institutions in the East are heavily concentrated in the old Northeast. Seventeen of the twenty-five private research universities are located northeast of a line drawn from Washington through Pittsburgh to Cleveland.

5.7 LEADING RESEARCH UNIVERSITIES, PUBLIC AND PRIVATE, 1987

PRIVATE ●

PUBLIC ▲

6

Two-Year Colleges

6.1 ENROLLMENT IN TWO-YEAR COLLEGES

A total of 5,083,461 students were enrolled in public community colleges and private two-year junior colleges in fall 1989. The full-time equivalent student total is 2,930,232. California stands out with 1,048,842 full- and part-time students in 139 two-year colleges, approximately 21 percent of the nation's two-year college enrollment in 1989. Other states that stand out on the map also have large populations, including New York, Florida, Michigan, Pennsylvania, Ohio, Illinois, and Texas. Private enrollment represents only 5 percent of total two-year enrollment, but it is important in six states that have more than 10,000 two-year students in private colleges: Pennsylvania, Ohio, New York, Massachusetts, California, and Georgia. Pennsylvania has the most two-year private college students, more than 37,000.

The relationship of enrollment in community colleges to population size can be more clearly seen when the two variables are compared. The seven states with more than 150,000 two-year college students are among the eight most populous states in the country. The extent of concentration of two-year college enrollment in the more populous states is dramatically illustrated by the fact that the ten most populous states have 63 percent of the nation's two-year college enrollment while having 54 percent of the nation's population.

Conversely, the relationship between states with small populations and small two-year college enrollments (fewer than 50,000 students) is striking: the twenty states with smallest enrollments include eighteen of the twenty least-populated states. One of these states, South Dakota, does not have a public two-year system, but it does have a single private junior college with 359 students. Montana, the smallest public system, has only 4,736 students, closely followed by Vermont with 4,798 students. The area on the map with the fewest two-year students is a bloc of eight states with small populations in the northern Great Plains, northern Rocky Mountain states, and in the Great Basin.

6.1 ENROLLMENT IN TWO-YEAR COLLEGES, 1989

STUDENTS

LESS THAN 50,000

50,000 TO 150,000

MORE THAN 150,000

121

6.2 PROPORTION OF ENROLLMENT IN TWO-YEAR COLLEGES

The proportion of total undergraduate enrollment in two-year and junior colleges (public and private institutions) varies greatly among the states. The largest proportions of enrollment in two-year colleges are found in six states where more than 50 percent of undergraduates attend two-year colleges. These states are concentrated in five states in the West: California, Nevada, Arizona, Washington, and Wyoming. Florida is also in the over 50 percent category, but the very highest proportions are in the far West: 57 percent in Washington, 57 percent in Arizona, and 60 percent in California.

States with an intermediate proportion of two-year college enrollment, 35 to 50 percent, are concentrated in a few areas. One contiguous bloc includes Oklahoma, Texas, New Mexico, Colorado, and Kansas. A second area is a portion of the Middle and South Atlantic, including the strip of states from New Jersey to North Carolina, except Delaware. Oregon, Michigan, Illinois, Mississippi, and Hawaii are the only other states in the intermediate category.

A large portion of the nation has less than 35 percent of undergraduates in two-year colleges. These states include all of New England, New York, and Pennsylvania, most of the Midwest, and the northern Great Plains, and northern Rocky Mountain states. Only 11 percent of Louisiana's enrollment is in two-year colleges; the state has six community colleges and four private junior colleges. South Dakota and Alaska have no public community college system, and only one percent of their undergraduate students is in two-year private colleges. These consist of a single private two-year college in Alaska and in South Dakota.

6.2 PROPORTION OF ENROLLMENT IN TWO-YEAR COLLEGES
(AS A PROPORTION OF UNDERGRADUATE ENROLLMENT, FALL 1989)

PERCENT

LESS THAN 35

35 TO 50

MORE THAN 50

123

6.3 AVERAGE ENROLLMENT AT COMMUNITY COLLEGES

Average enrollment at publicly supported community colleges tends to be highest in a few geographical areas. As data for only public two-year colleges were used to make this map, these figures reflect the average size of state campus systems. Two areas in which average community college size is greater than 5,000 students include the West Coast and adjacent Nevada, Utah, and Arizona; and four states of the Midwest: Wisconsin, Michigan, Missouri, and Illinois. Two Sunbelt states that have experienced recent growth in population stand out as well: Florida and Texas. Six East Coast states—Virginia, Maryland, Pennsylvania, New Jersey, New York, and Rhode Island—also have large average college size. It is important to note that these average figures are for entire community colleges; a large college may have several campuses of smaller size.

States with small college size (fewer than 2,500 students) tend to be located in a few regions. These include a band of Great Plains and Rocky Mountain states from Nebraska to North Dakota and from Minnesota to Montana, and a large arc of southern states from Arkansas to North Carolina. All of northern New England is in the smallest size category, as are two other states Kentucky, and New Mexico.

States with intermediate-size community colleges, those having 2,500 to 5,000 students, are scattered without any particular geographic pattern.

Generally, there is a tendency for the states with larger populations to have the largest average community college size. Eight of the ten most populous states are in the largest size category. However, one of the top ten, North Carolina, is in the smallest size category. Conversely, seven of the ten states with the smallest populations are also in the smallest average community college size category. Again there is an exception, as small Rhode Island has the highest average college size because it has a single community college, the Community College of Rhode Island, with about 15,400 students. Of course, in states with small populations there are often very few community colleges, so the average college size may reflect only one or two schools. The smallest average size is in sparsely populated Montana, where seven colleges have an average enrollment of fewer than 700 students.

6.3 AVERAGE ENROLLMENT AT COMMUNITY COLLEGES
(PUBLIC TWO-YEAR COLLEGES, FALL 1989)

STUDENTS

LESS THAN 2500

2500 TO 5000

MORE THAN 5000

* NOT APPLICABLE

6.4 NUMBER OF ASSOCIATE DEGREES GRANTED

The map showing the number of associate degrees awarded in one year bears a strong resemblance to simple population distribution and to other maps that primarily reflect population distribution, such as total enrollment. The states with the most population stand out most distinctly, especially California, New York, Texas, Florida, Illinois, and Michigan. Closer comparison of this map with population distribution, however, shows that there are states that stand out in the number of associate degrees even when population is taken into account. New York, for example, awarded almost 49,000 associate degrees, more than the approximately 48,500 awarded by California, despite California's edge in population. The main reason for this discrepancy is because in New York and several other states, large numbers of associate degrees are granted by four-year colleges. Thus the maps of two-year college enrollment and the map of associate degrees granted are not directly comparable. Other big states that appear to award more associate degrees than their population warrants are Michigan, Florida, and Washington. Comparison of this map with map 6.5 shows that the states mentioned do award a larger number of associate degrees per capita than most other states. At the other extreme from California and New York are states awarding a small number of degrees. Four states and the District of Columbia awarded between 400 and 1,000 associate degrees: Alaska, Montana, Nevada, and South Dakota. All five not only awarded very few associate degrees, but awarded relatively few of these degrees per capita.

6.4 NUMBER OF ASSOCIATE DEGREES GRANTED, 1989–90

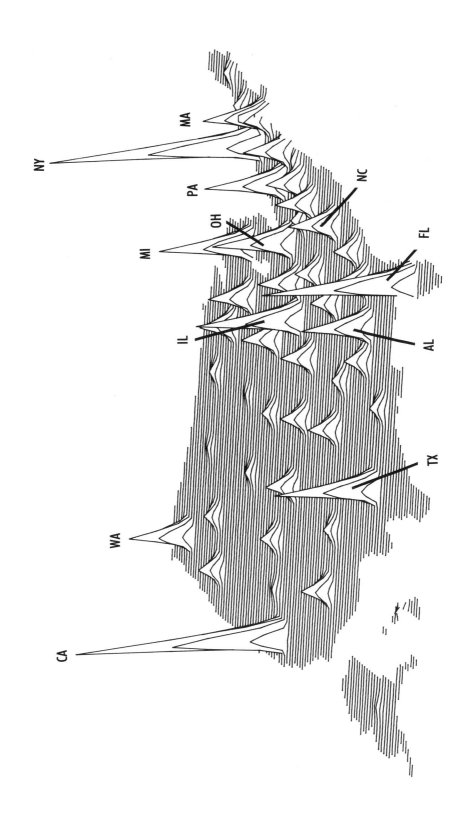

6.5 ASSOCIATE DEGREES AWARDED PER 10,000 POPULATION

It is difficult to generalize about the geographic pattern of associate degrees awarded per 10,000 population because of the lack of distinct regional blocs. There is a general tendency, however, for northern states across the width of the nation to award more associate degrees per 10,000 people and for the southern states to award fewer. For example, New York and four of the New England states (Massachusetts, Vermont, New Hampshire, and Rhode Island) awarded more than twenty associate degrees annually per 10,000 people. On the other hand, a number of states in the South, including Virginia, Tennessee, Georgia, Arkansas, Louisiana, and Texas, awarded fewer than fifteen degrees per 10,000 people. There were only two southern states in the highest category, Alabama and Florida, although the former had the highest ratio in the nation. Generally, states in the intermediate category were scattered without any particular pattern, although most of the Midwest fell into this class. The states with the highest ratio of associate degrees awarded per 10,000 population were Alabama (38), Wyoming (36), and Rhode Island (35). Louisiana had the lowest ratio, about six per 10,000 population, closely followed by the District of Columbia (7) and Nevada (8).

It is interesting to note that this band of northern states closely resembles the band of northern states on the map of community college tuition as a proportion of four-year in-state college tuition. Nine states in the northern half of the country with a high ratio of associate degrees awarded per capita are also states with relatively expensive community college tuition. As many of these are also states with high four-year college tuition, it may be that students still perceive these higher community college costs as a bargain compared to four-year costs.

6.5 ASSOCIATE DEGREES AWARDED PER 10,000 POPULATION, 1989–90

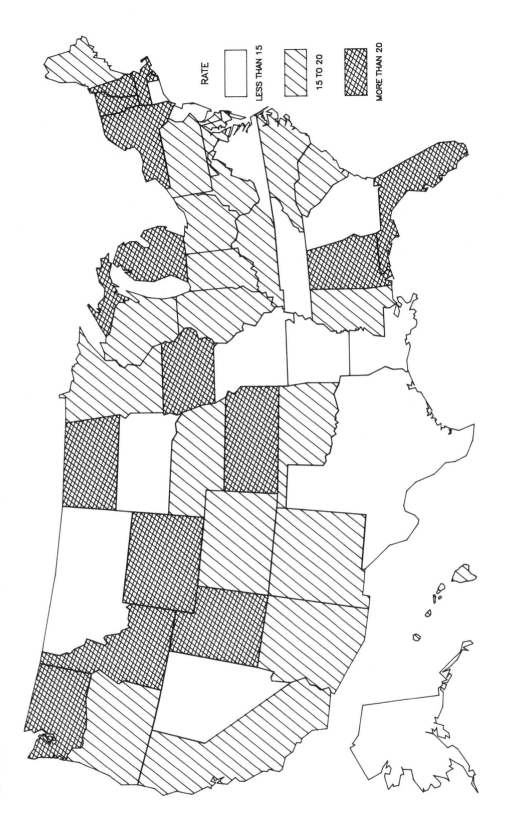

RATE

LESS THAN 15

15 TO 20

MORE THAN 20

6.6 TUITION AT PUBLIC TWO-YEAR COLLEGES

The geographic pattern of tuition at public two-year colleges (community colleges) can be described in a relatively simple manner. Tuition is highest (more than $1,000) in a northern band of states stretching from North Dakota through the upper Midwest and Great Lakes states to the northern Mid-Atlantic states and New England (except Connecticut). The highest community college tuition is in Vermont, where the average tuition is $2,210 annually. Vermont, which was also noted as having the highest average four-year tuition, is really in a class by itself as its two-year tuition far exceeds the next two highest states, Ohio and New Hampshire, which have costs of $1,636 and $1,608, respectively.

The states with the lowest two-year tuitions are located in a band from California through the desert Southwest to Texas. They form a band of states symmetrically opposite to the high-cost northern and northeastern band of states. North Carolina, and Hawaii are the only states with low two-year tuition outside this region. By far, the very lowest cost is in California, where community college tuition averages only $112. North Carolina is next at $228.

States in the middle category, $600 to $1,000, occupy an intermediate location between the two regions already described. They form a large, contiguous band of states stretching from the Northwest to the Southeast, from Washington state to Florida. The only medium-priced states outside this region are Connecticut and Delaware.

Comparison of the maps of public in-state tuition at two- and four-year institutions shows general similarities. On both maps, the states with higher tuition tend to be in the northern and northeastern parts of the country while the lower-cost states are located in the western and southwestern parts. There are two notable exceptions, however: New York and Utah. Both states have some of the highest average tuition costs for two-year colleges yet are among the lowest-cost states for four-year institutions.

6.6 TUITION AT PUBLIC TWO-YEAR COLLEGES
(AVERAGE UNDERGRADUATE TUITION, 1989–90)

DOLLARS

LESS THAN 600

600 TO 1000

MORE THAN 1000

*   NOT APPLICABLE

6.7 COMMUNITY COLLEGE TUITION AS A PROPORTION OF PUBLIC FOUR-YEAR COLLEGE IN-STATE TUITION

Community college tuition as a proportion of public four-year college in-state tuition tends to be highest in the northern half of the country. Community colleges include only public two-year institutions. Several clusters of states stand out: one in the West, including Idaho, Utah, and Wyoming; one in the northern Plains and Midwest, comprised of North Dakota, Nebraska, Minnesota, Iowa, and Wisconsin; one in the eastern Midwest, including Indiana and Ohio; and one in the Northeast, made up of New York, New Hampshire, Vermont, and Massachusetts. The only southern state on the map in this more than 60 percent category is Oklahoma. As on the map comparing two-year faculty salaries with four-year salaries, a relatively high figure may mean either that community college tuition is high or that four-year college tuition is low, so this map must be studied in conjunction with the maps showing overall patterns of two-year and four-year college tuition. Because the most distinctive feature of the community college tuition map was a broad swath of states with relatively high tuition charges across the northern half of the country, this generally means that a high figure on this proportional map indicates that community college tuition is relatively high. The highest ratio of two-year tuition to four-year tuition is in New York state (97%). New York is far above the next highest state, Utah (80%).

States where community college tuition is inexpensive relative to public four-year in-state tuition include Rhode Island and Delaware; all states of the Atlantic and Gulf Coast from Virginia to Mississippi, except Georgia; and several states in the West, including Oregon, California, Arizona, New Mexico, and Colorado. The state with the lowest ratio is California (9%). In this exceptional case, community college tuition was $112 in 1989–90 compared to $1,123 at four-year public colleges. The next lowest states are North Carolina (28%) and Delaware and Hawaii (32%). Unlike the highest and lowest categories, there is no distinct geographical pattern among the states in the intermediate category.

6.7 COMMUNITY COLLEGE TUITION AS A PROPORTION OF
PUBLIC FOUR-YEAR COLLEGE IN-STATE TUITION, 1989–90

PERCENT

LESS THAN 45

45 TO 60

MORE THAN 60

* NOT APPLICABLE

\# NOT AVAILABLE

6.8 AVERAGE FACULTY SALARY IN TWO-YEAR COLLEGES

Faculty salary data used on this map include both public and private two-year colleges. This map shows that there are three distinct clusters of states that pay two-year faculty at relatively high rates. The areas that pay their faculty more than $35,000 include a cluster of seven states in Megalopolis from Rhode Island and Connecticut through Maryland and Delaware. In this group, the highest-paying two-year colleges are in New York, which in 1989–90 paid their faculty an average of $41,292. A second cluster is in the Midwest, including Minnesota, Wisconsin, Michigan, and Illinois; the highest average salary in this group is in Michigan ($39,375). The third cluster is in the West, including California, Arizona, and Hawaii; here Arizona is highest at $37,413.

At the other extreme, there are large blocs of states that pay relatively low salaries (less than $28,000) to two-year faculty. Except for Wyoming, which stands out like an island in the interme-diate category, a huge bloc of eight western states, covering the northern Great Plains, the Rocky Mountain states, and several southwestern states, is in the lowest category. Other areas in the lowest category include the three states of the lower Mississippi River basin: Arkansas, Louisiana, and Mississippi. Both Carolinas, Indiana, Kentucky, and West Virginia, and outliers in Vermont are also in this category. The lowest average salary is in South Dakota, where two-year faculty earn an average of $21,000, although this statistic reflects one private junior college. The next lowest salaries are in West Virginia ($24,127) and Nebraska ($24,404).

Intermediate salaries, those in the range between $28,000 and $35,000, are recorded in a few geographic areas: in New England in Massachusetts, New Hampshire, and Maine; in four southeast-ern states; in Texas and four states in the southern Great Plains and central interior; and in the West in Washington, Oregon, and Nevada.

6.8 AVERAGE FACULTY SALARY IN TWO-YEAR COLLEGES, 1989–90

DOLLARS

LESS THAN 28,000

28,000 TO 35,000

MORE THAN 35,000

* NOT AVAILABLE

6.9 FACULTY SALARIES AT TWO-YEAR COLLEGES AS A PROPORTION OF SALARIES AT FOUR-YEAR COLLEGES

In its broad outline, this map, which includes data for both public and private institutions, bears a strong resemblance to the previous map which described average salaries at two-year colleges. A few states, especially in the Northeast and Midwest, pay their two-year faculty higher amounts, and many of those same states fall into the highest category on this map. In the highest category, two-year faculty receive at least 85 percent of the average salary of four-year faculty. Of course, the four-year-salary map must also be consulted because a high percentage on this map may simply indicate that four-year faculty are not well paid. Of the eleven states on this map in the 85 percent or above category, eight were also in the highest category on the previous map; the other three were in the intermediate category. Again, these states tend to be in the Northeast and Midwest, with the addition of Arizona, Oregon, and Alabama. The state with the highest proportion is Michigan, where two-year faculty earn an average of 94 percent of the salary of four-year faculty. Minnesota and Oregon are also high, both at 93 percent.

Similarly, states in the lowest salary category on map 6.8 also tend to be in the lowest category on this map. There is again a large bloc of nine states in the lowest category west of the Mississippi, from Iowa and the central Great Plains through the Rocky Mountain states. The two Carolinas, Arkansas, Louisiana, Indiana, and Kentucky stand out on this map as they did on the previous one. The states where two-year faculty compared to four-year faculty are paid the least are Indiana and North Carolina, both at 65 percent.

6.9 FACULTY SALARIES AT TWO-YEAR COLLEGES AS A PROPORTION OF SALARIES AT
FOUR-YEAR COLLEGES, 1989–90

PERCENT

☐ LESS THAN 80

▨ 80 TO 85

▨ MORE THAN 85

* NOT AVAILABLE

7

Outcomes of Higher Education

7.1 ADULTS WITH FOUR OR MORE YEARS OF COLLEGE

The U.S. Bureau of the Census regularly reports measures of educational achievement of the population, including proportions of the adult population who have graduated from high school or who have completed four years of college. A sample survey was taken in 1989. Percentages from this sample survey have been mapped, and they show considerable upward movement from the 1980 census. The 1989 map reflects very little change in regional patterns; it is simply that percentages for all states have moved upward.

Immediately apparent from the map is that there is a region of high attainment in the urban belt of the East Coast. States in the high category, where more than 23 percent of persons over twenty-five have completed four or more years of college, include Vermont, New Hampshire, Massachusetts, Connecticut, New Jersey, Maryland, and Virginia. The highest ranks were found in this area: all-urban Washington, D.C., ranked first with 35.2 percent, Massachusetts was second with 28.1 percent, and Connecticut was third with 27.5 percent. The only states in this urban region (which geographers commonly call Megalopolis) that dropped down into the second category were Maine, Rhode Island, Pennsylvania, New York, and Delaware. New York was barely below the chosen dividing line of 23 percent, and Rhode Island and Delaware had more than 19 percent. Two other regional groupings are apparent. Colorado and Utah constitute a Rocky Mountain high area, while California, Washington, Alaska, and Hawaii make up a Pacific region of high achievement.

Another outstanding feature is that most of the West falls at least into the middle level. All of the southern states except Virginia, Maryland, Texas, and Florida fall into the lowest category, with less than 18.5 percent of adults having attended four years of college. The Midwest also falls largely into this low category, with Illinois, Wisconsin, and Minnesota rising into the middle range.

7.1 ADULTS WITH FOUR OR MORE YEARS OF COLLEGE, 1989

PERCENT

LESS THAN 18.5

18.5 TO 23.0

MORE THAN 23.0

7.2 EDUCATIONAL ATTAINMENT: WHITES

The 1989 sample survey that provided data for the previous map also provided data on educational attainment of various subsets of the population. These data broken down by ethnicity and by gender were, however, available only by census region. Regional maps are therefore presented for whites, African-Americans, and Hispanics, as well as for men and for women.

A map of the regional attainment of white citizens of the U.S. might well be expected to coincide with the map for the total population, of which whites made up 80.3 percent, according to the 1990 census. That is, comparison with map 7.1 leads one to expect that levels of college attainment would be higher in the Northeast and West and lower in the Midwest and South. A look at the regional map of educational attainment by whites shows that this is indeed the case. The proportion of whites over twenty-five with four or more years of college is highest in the West census region (24.4%). Next is the Northeast (23.5%), followed by the South (21.0%). The Midwest is lowest with 19.2 percent.

7.2 EDUCATIONAL ATTAINMENT: WHITES
(PROPORTION OVER 25 WITH FOUR OR MORE YEARS OF COLLEGE, BY REGION, 1989)

PERCENT

Midwest 19.2

South 21.0

Northeast 23.5

West 24.4

7.3 EDUCATIONAL ATTAINMENT: AFRICAN-AMERICANS

Some differences are noted when the map of educational attainment of African-Americans is compared with the previous map on whites. It is similar in that the West is the area of highest achievement and the Northeast is next, although the percentages (18.6 and 13.3) are lower. The Midwest has the third largest proportion for African-Americans (11.3%), while the South was third for whites. The South, not unexpectedly, ranks last for African-Americans, with only 10.3 percent of adults over twenty-five having obtained college degrees. Comparing this map with some regional figures from the 1990 census shows that African-Americans have the lowest rate of college degree attainment in the region in which they make up the largest proportion of the population, that is, in the South, where they comprise 18.5 percent of the total population. They have the highest proportion of college graduates in the region in which they are least numerous, in the West, where they make up only 5.4 percent.

7.3 EDUCATIONAL ATTAINMENT: AFRICAN-AMERICANS
(PROPORTION OVER 25 WITH FOUR OR MORE YEARS OF COLLEGE, BY REGION, 1989)

PERCENT

South 10.3

Midwest 11.3

Northeast 13.3

West 18.6

7.4 EDUCATIONAL ATTAINMENT: HISPANICS

The regional map of Hispanics is the most striking of this series because it reverses the overall pattern. The Midwest is highest; here 12.3 percent of Hispanic adults have attained four or more years of college. The South is slightly behind with 12 percent, followed by the Northeast with 10.6 percent. But the West, which has been noted as having the highest educational attainment for both whites and blacks, is lowest for Hispanics, with only 7.6 percent of adults having gone to college for four or more years.

Two things should be noted when interpreting the map. One is that persons of Hispanic origin may be of any race; this is a linguistic category, not a racial one. The second is to look at the overall proportions of Hispanics in the population, as was done for African-Americans. The proportion of Hispanic college graduates is lowest in the region in which they are most numerous and highest in the region in which they make up the smallest proportion (Midwest). This was the same situation ascribed to African-Americans. Hispanics make up 19.1 percent of the population in the West, 7.9 percent in the South, 7.4 percent in the Northeast, and only 2.9 percent in the Midwest.

7.4 EDUCATIONAL ATTAINMENT: HISPANICS
(PROPORTION OVER 25 WITH FOUR OR MORE YEARS OF COLLEGE, BY REGION, 1989)

PERCENT

West 7.6

Northeast 10.6

South 12.0

Midwest 12.3

7.5 EDUCATIONAL ATTAINMENT: WOMEN

As in the case of ethnicity, there are regional differences in the higher educational achievement of males and females. The pattern for women is the same as the overall pattern for whites, in terms of regional ranking. Women in the West fare best: 21.5 percent of adult women have had four or more years of college. This is closely followed by the Northeast, with 19.9 percent. The South is next, with 16.6 percent, and the Midwest trails with only 15.8 percent.

7.5 EDUCATIONAL ATTAINMENT: WOMEN
(PROPORTION OVER 25 WITH FOUR OR MORE YEARS OF COLLEGE, BY REGION, 1989)

PERCENT

Midwest 15.8

South 16.6

Northeast 19.9

West 21.5

7.6 EDUCATIONAL ATTAINMENT: MEN

The map of educational attainment for men differs from that of women in that the Midwest and the South have exactly the same proportion of adult men over twenty-five with four or more years of college. In each of these regions, the sample data gave a percentage of 22.3, and these were the regions of lowest achievement. However, this low figure for men is higher than the highest figure for women, which was 21.5 percent in the West. The highest region for men is the West, where 28.3 percent of adult men have college degrees. The Northeast, as expected, is also high at 26.7 percent. The pattern for men is thus very much to be expected from the map of achievement of the total population by states—higher in the West and Northeast, lower in the South and Midwest. And, in all four regions, the percentage for men was higher than that for any other subset of the population examined.

Overall, the conclusions from the maps are that the West ranks highest, followed by the Northeast, for most groups; it is conspicuous in its low attainment for its Hispanic citizens. The South and Midwest rank lower than the other two regions, but differ from each other only slightly. Again, the difference is in Hispanics, who in terms of higher educational attainment fare far better in the Midwest than in any other region. This must be looked at against the background of the overall distribution of this subgroup of the population, as portrayed in the section on ethnic diversity.

7.6 EDUCATIONAL ATTAINMENT: MEN
(PROPORTION OVER 25 WITH FOUR OR MORE YEARS OF COLLEGE, BY REGION, 1989)

PERCENT

Midwest 22.3

South 22.3

Northeast 26.7

West 28.3

151

7.7 BACHELOR'S DEGREES AWARDED PER 10,000 POPULATION

This map shows the rate of baccalaureate degree attainment per 10,000 population, based on the number of degrees granted in each state during the 1989–90 school year. It is the first of a series of four such maps, and the unit of population is set at 10,000 in order to have whole numbers as rates for all four maps. (These rates are similar to other basic demographic rates, such as birth rates, death rates, or marriage and divorce rates.) This is a rather basic map, for the bachelor's degree is generally regarded as a standard measure of outcomes of higher education. The proportion of the population with "college degrees" usually means bachelor's degrees and higher; the census routinely reports the number and proportion of people with "four years or more of higher education."

The pattern on the map displays several areas with high rates of educational attainment. After the exceptionally high rate of 123 degrees per 10,000 for the District of Columbia—the usual urban anomaly with its many universities and colleges—several New England states rank very high. Rhode Island ranks second with 88, followed by Vermont with 80 and Massachusetts with 72. New Hampshire is seventh with a rate of 61. A large bloc of northern Plains states, with an extension into Colorado and Utah, forms the second area that has a high rate of granting bachelor's degrees. Within this group, rates range from 66 in North Dakota down to the low 50s in South Dakota and Wisconsin. The final pair of states in the high category are Delaware and Pennsylvania, also in the low 50s. The second category includes the largest number of states, well dispersed throughout the country, where 36 to 50 bachelor's degrees per 10,000 population were awarded. They include many of the industrial northeastern states.

In the lowest category, with rates of less than 36 per 10,000, are many scattered states. All except sparsely populated Idaho and Alaska are Sunbelt states, including large and rapidly growing Florida and California. Not surprisingly, it is Alaska, with its few colleges, that has the lowest rate of 19. It is more surprising that Florida granted only 27 bachelor's degrees per 10,000 in this year.

7.7 BACHELOR'S DEGREES AWARDED PER 10,000 POPULATION, 1989–90

RATE

LESS THAN 36

36 TO 50

MORE THAN 50

7.8 MASTER'S DEGREES AWARDED PER 10,000 POPULATION

For many people a master's degree represents the highest step on the ladder of higher educational attainment. It provides a professional credential in many fields, such as architecture and social work. The master's degrees in business administration and education are extremely popular. The map of master's degrees awarded per 10,000 population in the 1989–90 academic year differs considerably from the previous map of bachelor's degrees. The rates, of course, are generally much lower than those for bachelor's degrees. While the range of rates of baccalaureate degrees was from 19 to 88 (with 123 in Washington, D.C.), the range for master's degrees among the states was from a low of 6 in Maine and Alaska to a high of 30 in Massachusetts (with D.C. at 84).

It is noteworthy that the rate of awarding master's degrees is actually higher in Massachusetts than the rate of awarding bachelor's degrees in a few other states. New York ranked second with a rate of 21.

The regions of highest achievement are found in New York and New England. There are two other outlying areas with high rates, all at more than 13 degrees per 10,000 population: one includes Illinois, Michigan, and Missouri; another is Utah and Colorado, which were also ranked high in bachelor's degrees, plus neighboring Arizona. Finally, Maryland, which ranked eleventh with a rate of 14, is an outlying single state.

Middle category rates of 11–13 per 10,000 were found in the three West Coast states and in some northern, Midwest, and Great Plains states, as well as in a few scattered southern states. Generally, though, the states with low rates, less than 11 per 10,000, are found in the South and in a northern tier of Great Plains and Rocky Mountain states. Also in the low category are New Jersey and Maine. The state that ranked lowest in terms of awarding master's degrees was Nevada, with a rate of 5 per 10,000; Maine and Alaska ranked only slightly higher with 6.

7.8 MASTER'S DEGREES AWARDED PER 10,000 POPULATION, 1989–90

RATE

LESS THAN 11

11 TO 13

MORE THAN 13

7.9 DOCTORAL DEGREES AWARDED PER 10,000 POPULATION

Doctoral degrees included in the data mapped here are Ph.D.'s, Ed.D.'s, and other academic doctoral degrees. Medical, dental, and veterinary medical doctor's degrees are included on the map of professional degrees. The academic doctor's degrees comprise the smallest number of degrees awarded in a given year, and the number is more apt to fluctuate from year to year. The map can be used in conjunction with map 5.5, which shows the distribution of institutions that granted the largest numbers of doctor's degrees over a ten-year period.

Due to the small numbers, the map categories are very simple. There is a low category, where the rate of awarding doctor's degrees is less than 1 per 10,000 population, a middle category with rates of 1 to 1.5, and a high category with more than 1.5 degrees. The District of Columbia is by far the highest, with a rate of 8.8. Again confirming its specialization in higher education, Massachusetts is highest among the fifty states, with a rate of 3.5 per 10,000. Iowa and Colorado come next with rates of 2.2, followed by New York, Illinois, and Utah with rates of 2.1. No other states have rates above 2 per 10,000.

The map shows three regions of high achievement in terms of doctor's degrees (more than 1.5 per 10,000). First, there is a large northeastern region stretching from Massachusetts and Rhode Island westward to Iowa and Minnesota. Second, the states of Utah and Colorado fall into the high category (with quite high rates, as indicated). Third, there is another grouping of two states, California and Oregon, on the West Coast. In the lowest category are two northern New England states as well as West Virginia and Kentucky, Alabama and Arkansas. There are also four states in the West: Nevada, Idaho, Montana, and South Dakota. Alaska has the lowest rate, 0.1 doctoral degrees per 10,000. The many states in the middle category, where 1 to 1.5 degrees per 10,000 are granted, are widely dispersed throughout the country.

7.9 DOCTORAL DEGREES AWARDED PER 10,000 POPULATION, 1989–90

RATE

LESS THAN 1.0

1.0 TO 1.5

MORE THAN 1.5

7.10 PROFESSIONAL DEGREES AWARDED PER 10,000 POPULATION

The map of first professional degrees should be looked at in conjunction with the maps of medical schools, law schools, dental schools, and veterinary medical schools. First professional degrees are those requiring at least six years of college work, including a minimum of two years of professional training. Such degrees include law, medicine, theology, dentistry, veterinary medicine, chiropractic medicine, pharmacy, optometry, osteopathic medicine, and podiatry. In other words, they include the fields that have traditionally been defined as the professions—law, theology, and medicine, including many associated health-care specialties. Rates of first professional degrees are somewhat higher than those for doctoral degrees. Excluding the anomalous high rate of 40.6 for the District of Columbia, however, they range from a high of 6.1 in Massachusetts to a low of 0.4 in Nevada (Alaska awarded none).

This map is somewhat different from the preceding three, which had some features in common. On the East Coast, only Massachusetts, New York, and Delaware fall into the top category. Utah and Colorado, in the highest category on all three other maps, have fallen to the low category. Louisiana appears on the map, the first southern state to be in the high category on any of the maps. Five states comprising a bloc in the heartland of the country also fall into the high category; they include Illinois, Iowa, Minnesota, Nebraska, and Missouri. Perhaps the most outstanding difference is that so many western states, all except California, Oregon, and Oklahoma, fall into the low category. This situation is made clearer by comparing this map to the maps of various kinds of professional schools (law, medicine, dentistry, and veterinary medicine) in chapter 5.

7.10 PROFESSIONAL DEGREES AWARDED PER 10,000 POPULATION, 1989–90

RATE

LESS THAN 2.5

2.5 TO 3.4

MORE THAN 3.4

8

Student Costs and Student Aid

8.1 TOTAL COSTS AT PUBLIC COLLEGES

The total average yearly cost of education for students at public four-year colleges ranges from a high of $7,715 in Vermont to a low of $3,509 in Kansas for the 1989–90 academic year. These costs include in-state tuition, fees, and room and board. Regionally, the interior and southern parts of the United States have the lowest average total costs while the Northeast and West Coast have the highest.

Vermont is the state with the highest cost, in large part a reflection of the high cost at the University of Vermont. Another bloc of high-cost states, over $5,500, is located in the Mid-Atlantic and the eastern Midwest. Michigan, Ohio, Pennsylvania, New Jersey, Maryland, Delaware, and Virginia are the contiguous states that made up this bloc. The only other states with total costs over $5,500 are Rhode Island, California, and Arizona.

The states with intermediate total costs, $4,500 to $5,500, are primarily in the North and Northeast or contiguous to the bloc of highest-cost states. New York and all the remaining New England states fall into this category, as do Illinois, Indiana, and West Virginia. Five western states are also in this group, including Washington, Oregon, Montana, Colorado, and Hawaii. Minnesota and South Carolina are the only two remaining intermediate-cost states.

The remaining states have average total costs below $4,500. Almost half of the nation, twenty-four states, is in this huge bloc covering most of the South, the interior, and much of the West. With the exception of South Carolina and a bloc of four states from West Virginia east to Delaware, all of the South falls into this class. Alaska is in this category, as are all of the Great Plains and Rocky Mountain states except Montana and Colorado. Several midwestern states are included: Wisconsin, Iowa, and Missouri.

8.1 TOTAL COSTS AT PUBLIC COLLEGES
(PUBLIC FOUR-YEAR COLLEGES AND UNIVERSITIES, 1989–90)

COST

LESS THAN $4500

$4500 TO $5500

MORE THAN $5500

* NOT AVAILABLE

8.2 TOTAL COSTS AT PRIVATE COLLEGES

The North and the West Coast have the highest average total costs at private four-year colleges. Outside these two regions only Colorado and Louisiana have costs above $11,000 per year. In the North, only Michigan interrupts a solid bloc of high-cost states stretching from Minnesota to the Atlantic. Private colleges are most costly in Massachusetts, where the annual average is $16,904, and in Connecticut, where the average is $16,184. Louisiana's high ranking is due to the cost of numerous Catholic colleges in the state.

States with medium private college costs, $9,500 to $11,000, tend to be in the eastern half of the country. Of eleven such states, only Idaho and New Mexico are in the West. It should be noted that in these two states and in several other less populated states, there are relatively few private colleges, so the average figures are largely influenced by just a few colleges. For example, other than technical schools, business colleges, and Bible colleges, Wyoming has no four-year private colleges; Nevada has one (Sierra Nevada College); North Dakota, three; Idaho, three; and Alaska, two.

Private college total costs are lowest (less than $9,500) in the Deep South (South Carolina, Mississippi, and Alabama, and also Arkansas), Texas and the Great Plains, the northern Rocky Mountain states, and the Southwest. A few other states are also in the lowest category: Delaware, Kentucky, South Carolina, Alaska, and Hawaii. The lowest average total cost of private colleges is in Utah, where private school tuition averages $4,970. Indeed, private costs in Utah are so low that the state has the lowest differential between public and private college costs of all the states: $628. Utah's costs average $4,342 for public colleges and $4,970 for private colleges. Utah has only two private four-year colleges: Brigham Young University (Latter-Day Saints) and Westminster College of Salt Lake City (run by three Protestant denominations). The next lowest average total cost for private schools, $6,110, is in Arkansas, which has ten private colleges.

8.2 TOTAL COSTS AT PRIVATE COLLEGES
(PRIVATE FOUR-YEAR COLLEGES AND UNIVERSITIES, 1989–90)

COST

LESS THAN $9500

$9500 TO $11,000

MORE THAN $11,000

* NOT APPLICABLE

NOT AVAILABLE

8.3 IN-STATE TUITION

The map of in-state tuition is closely related, but not identical, to the map of total cost at public institutions. Generally, northern and eastern states have higher in-state tuition costs while southern and western states have lower ones.

The states with the very highest annual in-state tuition, more than $2,000, are mainly in the East. All the New England states except Maine are in this category. The four Mid-Atlantic states—Virginia, Pennsylvania, New Jersey, and Delaware—are also in this category, as are Ohio, Michigan, Minnesota, and Illinois. Eight of these states are also in the highest total college cost category. South Carolina is the only other state in the highest tuition category. Vermont is the state with the highest in-state tuition, $3,641, which represents almost half (47%) of the average Vermont total public college cost.

Most of the states in the next highest category, between $1,500 and $2,000, are located in the West and South. Several of these states were also in the intermediate categories of total college costs. There is a distinct bloc of states in the Deep South in the $1,500 to $2,000 tuition category: Louisiana, Mississippi, Alabama, and Georgia. The Midwest and northern Great Plains and Pacific Northwest states tend to have higher tuition costs than areas south of these regions. Most remarkable on the entire map are California and Arizona, with very low tuition ($1,123 and $1,362, respectively) but with high total costs, as was seen on the earlier map. California and Arizona's low tuition is more than offset by very high room-and-board fees: $4,424 and $4,233 in the two states, respectively. Arizona's board rates are particularly high ($2,817). Not only are they the highest in the country, but they are 26 percent higher than California, the next highest state.

States with the lowest in-state tuition are clustered in the South and West. In fact, with the exception of Colorado, the whole Southwest quadrant of the country is in this category. Although New York has the very lowest tuition in the North ($1,460), it is in the high total cost category. This is due to New York's relatively expensive room-and-board costs.

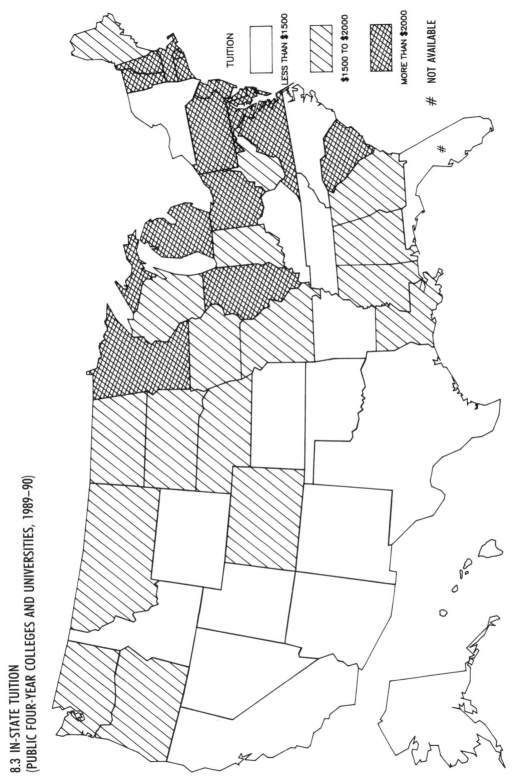

8.3 IN-STATE TUITION
(PUBLIC FOUR-YEAR COLLEGES AND UNIVERSITIES, 1989–90)

TUITION

LESS THAN $1500

$1500 TO $2000

MORE THAN $2000

\#   NOT AVAILABLE

8.4 TUITION AT PRIVATE COLLEGES

Average tuition at private colleges shows distinct regional patterns. The Northeast and the West Coast states are more costly than the rest of the country. In particular, the six New England states form a bloc of highest-cost states. Massachusetts, with an average tuition of $11,450, is highest, followed by Connecticut at $11,268. These two states were also highest in *total* costs at private colleges.

Intermediate tuition costs are found at private schools in the North (except Michigan), Colorado, and Louisiana, and in the three West Coast states. The rest of the country, including Alaska and Hawaii, has private tuition costs averaging less than $7,500. The lowest tuition costs are in Utah and Arkansas, which also had the lowest total costs. All in all, the maps of tuition at private colleges and total costs at private colleges show fairly similar regional patterns.

8.4 TUITION AT PRIVATE COLLEGES
(PRIVATE FOUR-YEAR COLLEGES AND UNIVERSITIES, 1989–90)

TUITION

LESS THAN $7500

$7500 TO $10,000

MORE THAN $10,000

*   NOT APPLICABLE

8.5 RATIO OF PRIVATE TO PUBLIC COLLEGE COSTS

The ratio of private to public college costs is a measure comparing private college and university costs within a state and public college costs in the same state. Costs include tuition, fees, room, and board and are for four-year institutions only. Given that more than 80 percent of students attend college in their home states, the information is of interest to the student or the parents of students comparing the relative costs of public and private schools within a state.

With few exceptions, not much of a regional pattern is shown on the map. The New York–New England region stands out in having relatively high-cost private schools compared to the cost of public colleges, although Vermont and Rhode Island are exceptions to the regional pattern.

States in the intermediate category—those where private costs are from two to two and a half times as much as public costs—include many of the interior states of the nation. They form two broad bands. One extends from the Mid-Atlantic states (excluding Delaware and Virginia, which have a ratio of less than 2), across the Midwest to South Dakota and Nebraska. These last two states also form part of the second band, a region sprawling across the Great Plains all the way to Texas. In addition to these blocs, Alaska, Oregon, and Washington fall into this category, as do three southern states: Tennessee, Alabama, and Georgia.

It is interesting to compare this map with the maps of total costs at public and private colleges. Some states have a small differential between public and private costs because public institutions are relatively expensive, as was noted in the case of Vermont, which has the highest public college costs. A small differential may also occur because private schools in an area are relatively inexpensive, which brings them close to public school costs. This is the case with Kentucky, Arkansas, and Mississippi. On the other hand, large differentials occur when a state has a high average cost at private institutions and a low average cost at public ones, such as Louisiana. Such cases are rare, implying that market factors are at work that allow private schools to charge more as public college costs increase in the home state and, conversely, that allow public costs to be raised as local private costs rise. In the majority of the states with a large differential between public and private tuition, however, the differential occurs because private college costs are simply so much greater than public costs. This is the case in the New York–New England region, and in California and Colorado.

8.5 RATIO OF PRIVATE TO PUBLIC COLLEGE COSTS
(FOUR-YEAR INSTITUTIONS: TUITION, FEES, ROOM, AND BOARD, 1989–90)

RATIO

☐ LESS THAN 2

▨ 2 TO 2.5

▩ MORE THAN 2.5

* NOT APPLICABLE

8.6 STATE SPENDING PER STUDENT FOR UNDERGRADUATE STUDENT AID

Need-based aid to undergraduates accounts for 88 percent of all student aid. The regional pattern of state spending for undergraduate need-based student aid is quite striking when aid is calculated per student. States in the northeastern quadrant of the country, from Minnesota and Iowa to southern New England, stand out in spending more than $100 per student. Of the fifteen states in this category, all are in the North except for South Carolina. Only New Hampshire and Maine are exceptions to a solid regional bloc. The state with the highest amount per capita is New York, at $462 per student. In fact, New York's program is so extensive that it accounts for one-quarter of the nation's undergraduate need-based aid. New Jersey and Vermont are also heavy spenders on undergraduate student aid, with over $300 per student.

Intermediate amounts of aid per student, $40 to $100, are spent on the West Coast and in an east-west band of states through the center of the nation from Colorado and New Mexico to West Virginia and Maryland. Less than $40 per student is spent in the remaining states, including a large bloc of western states in the northern Great Plains, northern Rocky Mountains, and Southwest. Another region of low spending is located in much of the South in a band from Texas to Georgia, as well as in Florida, Virginia, North Carolina, and Delaware. The states with the lowest average spending per student (between $6 and $9) are Alaska, Idaho, and Nevada.

8.6 STATE SPENDING PER STUDENT FOR UNDERGRADUATE STUDENT AID, 1989–90

DOLLARS

LESS THAN 40

40 TO 100

MORE THAN 100

8.7 GRANTS TO STUDENTS AS A PERCENTAGE OF STATE TAX FUNDS

Of state funds for higher education, the proportion devoted to student grants varies from 19 percent in Vermont and 14 percent in New York to less than one-half of one percent in Hawaii, Wyoming, Nevada, Montana, Idaho, and Mississippi. Generally, states in the North, and particularly in the Northeast, devote a larger share of their revenues to this purpose. In fact, all nine states devoting more than 7 percent of state higher-education funds to student grants are in the North. Seven of these states form a distinct cluster that includes Vermont, the three states of southern New England, New York, Pennsylvania, and New Jersey. Illinois and Minnesota are the only other states in this category.

The intermediate group, those states devoting 3 to 7 percent of their higher-education appropriations to student grants, includes the rest of the North, except for Maine and New Hampshire. Two adjacent states, Kentucky and West Virginia, are also in this group. Three South Atlantic states fall into this category: North Carolina, South Carolina, and Florida. A third intermediate group is the bloc of contiguous states composed of Texas, Oklahoma, New Mexico, Colorado, and Utah.

Those states devoting less than 3 percent of state higher-education funds to student grants are also distributed in regional clusters. In New England they are Maine and New Hampshire; in the Mid-Atlantic: Delaware, Maryland, and Virginia. A bloc of six southern states clustered about the Deep South is also included. With the exception of the five western states noted in the intermediate category, all western states, including Alaska and Hawaii, devote less than 3 percent of higher education funds to student grants.

8.7 GRANTS TO STUDENTS AS A PERCENTAGE OF STATE TAX FUNDS, 1990–91

PERCENT

LESS THAN 3

3 TO 7

MORE THAN 7

9

Financing of Higher Education

9.1 STATE APPROPRIATIONS PER FTE STUDENT AT PUBLIC INSTITUTIONS

This map shows the amounts that state and local governments appropriated for higher education per FTE student in 1988–89. Alaska, with its high cost of living, ranks first with $9,879 appropriated per student. The totally urban District of Columbia ranks second ($7,695), and Hawaii, with a high cost of living like Alaska, ranks third ($7,458). Of the contiguous forty-eight states, the largest concentration of states with relatively high appropriations (more than $4,500) are in the Northeast. This bloc of states includes New York, New Jersey, the three states of southern New England, and Delaware and Maine. Three Sunbelt states—California, Florida, and New Mexico—are also in this category, as is Wyoming.

The lowest category of appropriations, less than $3,750, is found among a broad band of states including Montana, all the states of the Great Plains, and the states of the lower Mississippi River basin. New Hampshire and Vermont, and several states of the eastern Midwest, are also in this category. Vermont ($2,337) is the lowest-ranked state, followed by Louisiana ($2,598).

Because of the swath of Great Plains states with very low appropriations per student, states in the intermediate range, $3,750 to $4,500, are concentrated in the eastern and western parts of the country. The Middle and South Atlantic from Pennsylvania to Georgia, the northern Midwest, and the states west of the Rockies fall largely into this category.

9.1 STATE APPROPRIATIONS PER FTE STUDENT AT PUBLIC INSTITUTIONS, 1988–89

DOLLARS

LESS THAN 3750

3750 TO 4500

MORE THAN 4500

9.2 PROPORTION OF GENERAL EXPENDITURES SPENT ON HIGHER EDUCATION

This map shows the proportion of a state's general expenditures that was spent for higher education in 1988–89. There was not much difference among the states in the proportions spent: the highest-ranked state, Kansas, spent 9 percent, and the lowest-ranked state, Vermont, spent 2 percent. This narrow range allows three very simple classes to be defined: those states spending approximately 6 percent of their general expenditures; those spending less; and those spending more.

The eighteen states spending more than 6 percent of general expenditures for higher education tend to be in the West or South. Twelve of the eighteen are west of the Mississippi River and they include a scattered group of states from the Great Plains, the Rocky Mountains, the Southwest, and California and Hawaii. There is a cluster in the northern Midwest (Minnesota, Wisconsin, and Iowa), and a southern cluster made up of Virginia, North Carolina, Tennessee, Georgia, and Alabama.

States that spend less than 6 percent of general expenditures on higher education tend to be concentrated in the northeastern quadrant of the country. Thirteen of these twenty states stretch in a contiguous band from Kentucky northeast to encompass all of New England. In addition to this large cluster, there are clusters in Montana and the Dakotas, and Arkansas and Louisiana. Alaska and Nevada are the remaining states in this lowest category; the latter stands out as an island surrounded by states in the highest category.

Unlike the highest and lowest categories, there is no particular geographic pattern to the states in the intermediate category—those spending approximately 6 percent of general expenditures for higher education. The only group that approaches a regional cluster is made up of four states in the Midwest stretching from Missouri through Illinois and Indiana to Michigan.

The explanation for the distribution shown on the map may lie mainly in regional patterns of total state spending. While the states of the Northeast have a reputation for high tax rates and high levels of expenditure, there are so many claims on the state dollar that higher education is a relatively small percentage of expenditures in these states. In states with a narrower range of expenditures, higher education receives a larger proportion of these expenditures. There is also an obvious connection between total cost at public colleges (map 8.1) and the proportion of expenditures spent on higher education, as a comparison of the two maps shows. Most notable is the correspondence between low proportion of general expenditures and high public college costs in the Northeast. Indeed, Vermont, already noted as the state with the lowest ranking on this map, is the state with the most expensive public college costs. At the other extreme, Kansas spends the largest proportion of its budget on higher education, and it is also the most inexpensive state in terms of total college costs.

9.2 PROPORTION OF GENERAL EXPENDITURES SPENT ON HIGHER EDUCATION, 1988–89

PERCENT

LESS THAN 6

6

MORE THAN 6

9.3 INCREASE IN PUBLIC HIGHER-EDUCATION FUNDING

This map shows the percentage increase in public higher-education expenditures over the five-year interval from 1982–83 to 1987–88. During this time, in the nation as a whole, higher education experienced a 47 percent average increase in expenditures. States with increases of more than 50 percent were concentrated in the eastern half of the nation, especially in the Southeast. Of twelve such states, eleven were east of the Great Plains; in the West, only Nevada had an increase of this magnitude. The eastern states with more than a 50 percent increase included all of the South Atlantic states from Virginia to Florida and the inland states of Tennessee, Alabama, and Arkansas. Only four states outside this region had large increases. Three of these were in the Northeast: Massachusetts, Connecticut, and New Jersey. The other was Nevada. The states with the largest increases were Massachusetts (80%) and Tennessee (68%).

States with the next highest level of increased funding, 40.1 to 50 percent, were in the northeastern and southwestern quadrants of the country. The four remaining New England states and California, Utah, and Arizona were in this category.

Next, in the 30 to 40 percent category, was a broad band of states stretching east-west across the center of the nation from Kentucky to Colorado and New Mexico. New York and the three Northwest states—Washington, Oregon, and Idaho—belonged to this group.

Eleven states had less than a 30 percent increase. One cluster of these states was made up of Montana, Wyoming, and the Dakotas; another cluster was Texas, Oklahoma, Louisiana, and Mississippi. Alaska, Hawaii, and West Virginia were also in this category. The states with the smallest increases were Alaska (4%), West Virginia (11%), and Oklahoma (13%).

9.3 INCREASE IN PUBLIC HIGHER-EDUCATION FUNDING
(PERCENT CHANGE, 1982–83 TO 1987–88)

PERCENT

LESS THAN 30.0

30.0 TO 40.0

40.1 TO 50.0

OVER 50.0

9.4 TOTAL FEDERAL FUNDING OF HIGHER EDUCATION

The map of total federal funding reflects 1988 federal obligations to colleges and universities. The amount of funding involved was huge—approximately $17.5 billion in 1988, or enough to finance about 350 medium-sized colleges with annual budgets of $50 million each.

The most striking aspect of the distribution of federal funding is the extent to which the bulk of funding was concentrated in a few states. California alone received $3.4 billion, and New York $1.5 billion. Massachusetts and Illinois received approximately $1 billion each, followed by four states with about $750 million each: Maryland, Pennsylvania, Texas, and New Mexico. In total, these eight states received slightly more than $10 billion, or 57 percent of all federal higher-education funding, even though they have only 40 percent of the national population. While there are some cases of large amounts allocated to special projects at particular universities, such as the Applied Physics Laboratory at Johns Hopkins, the general pattern follows closely the pattern of distribution of larger, more established schools, especially those that enroll large numbers of graduate students in doctoral programs. It is these students who are supported as research assistants on federal grants and who engage in much of the research supported by federal dollars. The remaining overall pattern generally follows that of total enrollment and, indirectly, of population distribution. Outside of the eight states listed above, the states of the Great Plains, northern Rocky Mountains, northern New England, and Alaska received relatively low levels of funding. States in the Midwest, South, and Pacific Northwest received middle levels of funding.

9.4 TOTAL FEDERAL FUNDING OF HIGHER EDUCATION
(FEDERAL OBLIGATIONS TO COLLEGES AND UNIVERSITIES, 1988)

185

9.5 REVENUES FROM FEDERAL GRANTS AND CONTRACTS

Much federal funding of higher education comes to colleges and universities from federal agencies in the way of grants and contracts for faculty to engage in research. This map shows the relative grant activity of faculty in each state by showing total federally funded research dollars in 1986–87 divided by the number of full-time faculty.

There were two areas of the country where institutions received an average of more than $25,000 in federal funds per faculty member: New England and the West, especially the West Coast and the Southwest. Three New England states were in this highest category: Massachusetts, Connecticut, and Vermont. In the West the states included California, Oregon, Washington, Nevada, Utah, Colorado, and New Mexico. Alaska and Hawaii were also in this category. Maryland and North Carolina were the only states in this category outside of these two regions.

States in the intermediate category, $15,500 to $25,000 per faculty member, were concentrated in a large bloc in the North stretching from North Dakota to New York and from Missouri to Pennsylvania. Only a few states lay outside of this bloc: Arizona, New Hampshire, and four states in the South (Tennessee, Alabama, Georgia, and Florida).

States in the lowest category, less than $15,500, also formed a fairly contiguous bloc through the northern Rocky Mountain states, the Great Plains, and the states of the lower Mississippi River basin. Maine, New Jersey, and a group of states made up of Indiana, Kentucky, West Virginia, and Virginia were in this category as well.

The distribution shown on this map partly comes about because of the pattern of federal funding of universities. In some cases the inclusion of a state in the highest category is guaranteed because of the presence of one or two universities that traditionally receive large amounts of federal funding such as Johns Hopkins in Maryland and MIT in Massachusetts.

Still, the overall pattern was biased toward the Northeast, North, and West Coast, with the interior of the nation and most southern states receiving much less federal funding per faculty member.

9.5 REVENUES FROM FEDERAL GRANTS AND CONTRACTS
(PER FULL-TIME FACULTY MEMBER, 1986–87)

DOLLARS

LESS THAN 15,500

15,500 TO 25,000

MORE THAN 25,000

9.6 INSTITUTIONS WITH THE LARGEST ENDOWMENTS

Universities with large endowments tend to be private institutions. Only three of the top twenty in 1989 were public institutions, and one of those, the second largest with about $3.7 billion in endowments, was the University of Texas system. Many of the forty institutions are also ones that are heavily involved in graduate education. The concentration in the North, particularly the Northeast and Midwest, is partly explained by the fact that schools with large endowments tend to be the older established schools, many of which are private and many of which are among the oldest established universities in the nation.

Of the forty schools with endowments of more than $300 million, only fourteen lie outside the Northeast and Midwest. Even within the Northeast and Midwest, the institutions are concentrated in a few states. New York has five, Massachusetts four, Ohio three, and Illinois three. Outside of these regions the only significant concentration of highly endowed universities are in California and Texas, which have three and five respectively. There is a vast area of the country from the Great Plains to the West Coast within which, with the exception of the eight schools in California and Texas, no other schools are on the map.

In addition to this regional concentration, universities with large endowments tend to be clustered in urban areas. Several urban areas are home to more than one institution. These include Boston, which has the institution with the largest endowment (Harvard, approximately $4.7 billion), and Wellesley College; New York City with Columbia, Rockefeller, and New York universities; Chicago with the University of Chicago, Northwestern, and Loyola; Philadelphia with the University of Pennsylvania and Swarthmore; and Los Angeles with Cal Tech and the University of Southern California.

9.6 INSTITUTIONS WITH THE LARGEST ENDOWMENTS
(ASSETS OF JUNE 30, 1991)

189

9.7 RECIPIENTS OF THE MOST FEDERAL FUNDING FOR RESEARCH AND DEVELOPMENT

Like institutions with the largest endowments, colleges and universities with the most federal funding are concentrated in the northeastern quadrant of the country, but there is also a large concentration in California. Of the twenty schools that received more than $100 million in 1989, six were in California and twelve were in the North. Only two schools, the University of Washington and Duke University, were outside these two areas.

While the geographical patterns of the two maps are similar, there is only a partial correspondence between the two sets of colleges. About half of the schools on this map were among the top forty schools in endowments. These are the very prestigious private research universities, specifically Johns Hopkins, Stanford, MIT, Columbia, Yale, Cornell, Pennsylvania, Duke, Washington University of St. Louis, and the University of Southern California. Johns Hopkins is the leader with $412 million in funding (much of it due to the Applied Physics Research Lab). Stanford and MIT are second and third with $240 million and $207 million, respectively.

The second half of this list, schools generally not appearing among the top forty in endowments, is made up of the big flagship schools of state systems. The Universities of Washington, Michigan, Wisconsin (Madison), and Minnesota and Penn State University fall into this category. Four schools of the University of California system are here as well: Los Angeles, San Diego, San Francisco, and Berkeley.

Because of the close relationship between research and development, doctoral programs, and graduate students, the schools on this map also contribute to the patterns that emerge on the maps of federal funding by state, specialization in graduate students, doctoral recipients, and grant revenues per faculty member.

190

9.7 RECIPIENTS OF THE MOST FEDERAL FUNDING FOR RESEARCH AND DEVELOPMENT, 1989

10

Summary

We conclude with a brief summary of major findings and a look at the status of higher education in the fifty states. The maps that have been presented confirm our belief that our country, with its fifty different state education systems plus a diversity of private colleges and universities, is too complex to be understood simply in terms of facts and figures. Maps help to understand the regional patterns that exist in higher education, as well as in politics, culture, and economy. Some maps, such as those showing various kinds of enrollment, mirror population distribution. But other maps, definitely different, show regional distinctions.

MAJOR FINDINGS

Enrollment

Total enrollment is closely correlated with population, although the states in the North and West have higher ratios of enrollment per capita. Enrollment growth parallels population growth. Private enrollment is more concentrated in the eastern half of the country, especially in New York, Massachusetts, and Pennsylvania. Massachusetts has the highest proportion of private enrollment at 67 percent, and, along with New York and Rhode Island, students in its private colleges outnumber those in public colleges.

Graduate enrollment is concentrated in these same three states (New York, Massachusetts, and Pennsylvania) as well as in Illinois, Michigan, and Ohio. Eight states have more than 60 percent of the nation's graduate enrollment. The Megalopolis states have the highest proportion of graduate enrollment to total enrollment and also the highest proportion of private graduate enrollment to total graduate enrollment.

Part-time enrollment is concentrated in the more urbanized states. Women make up the majority of full-time enrollment in the eastern half of the country, and they make up the majority of part-time enrollment in forty-nine states. Part-time female enrollment is also closely related to level of urbanization.

Campuses with the largest total enrollments are concentrated in the Midwest and the Southwest, particularly in Arizona. Small average campus sizes are often found in states with small populations.

Students and Faculty

A demographic measure—number of college students per 10,000 people—was mapped to determine whether college students are distributed equally in proportion to the total population. The map shows that three New England states, three western states, and two Great Plains states have the highest ratio of enrollment to population. In trying to analyze this ratio, it becomes obvious that it is highly related to in-migration and out-migration of students. A map of the sex ratio of entering freshmen is more simple in its regional pattern; males tend to predominate only in the West. The proportion of freshmen who are in-state residents is understood by examining maps of in-migration, out-migration, and net migration. Thirty states have more freshmen coming in than migrating out, but for many states the amount of net migration is very small. Although large numbers of students are involved in the migration, the in- and out- figures sometimes cancel each other out.

Five maps examine the distribution of bachelor's degrees granted in certain fields: business, agriculture, engineering, education, and social sciences.

Average faculty salary is highest in the states of Megalopolis, the Midwest, and in some western states, particularly in California. Midwestern universities tend to have the highest differential between male and female faculty salaries, while western ones have the lowest. The highest student-faculty ratios are in the Northeast, the Great Plains, and the West.

Cultural Diversity

This set of maps shows the geography of minorities in higher education; first the minority share of total enrollment, then enrollment of specific groups. For African-Americans, both the highest percentages of total enrollment, as well as the largest number of traditionally black colleges and universities, are found in the South and in certain northern urban areas. The distribution of blacks in higher education thus reflects the overall distribution of the black population. The same generalization is shown for Hispanics, who are concentrated in the Southwest but are also well represented in some urban areas. It is interesting that most of the institutions designated as being Hispanic-serving are public two-year institutions. Native Americans enter higher education only in small numbers, and they are concentrated in Alaska and in the contiguous states with Indian reservations. A relatively small number of tribally controlled colleges for American Indians are concentrated in these same states. The Asian pattern is not as distinct as the others, and there is no category of colleges specifically designated as Asian-American serving. However, Asians now constitute large percentages of students in many colleges in California and elsewhere.

Specialized Institutions

The distribution of law schools closely follows the distribution of population. All states have law schools in the public system, and private law schools are also widely distributed. Medical schools are fewer in number; they also are roughly distributed according to population, but they are mostly drawn to urban areas. Although law schools may be in "college towns," medical schools are usually in cities. Dental schools, though there are fewer of them, are almost always co-located with medical schools. Veterinary schools have a different distribution; there are only twenty-seven in the country, and only one state, Alabama, has two. States without veterinary medical schools have agreements with certain out-of-state schools to accept their students. Colorado has an example of a veterinary medical school that serves a large, sparsely populated area.

In addition to the professional schools, maps are presented that show the institutions granting the largest numbers of doctoral degrees in a recent ten-year period, those that have the largest university research libraries, and those that are the leading research universities, public and private, as classified by the Carnegie Foundation for the Advancement of Teaching in 1987. In all of these maps, there is a pronounced concentration of institutions in the Northeastern quadrant of the country.

Two-Year Colleges

California dominates community college enrollment with more than a million students, or 21 percent of the nation's community college enrollment. The proportion of students attending two-year colleges is highest in the West, particularly in California, where 60 percent of undergraduates attend these schools. Arizona and Washington also have a very large relative concentration of community college enrollment. Some states have tiny systems; two states, Alaska and South Dakota, do not have public two-year colleges.

The West Coast and the Midwest have the largest average size community colleges. In general, states with large populations have large average college size. The number of associate degrees granted per capita is highest in the North and lowest in the South. Tuition is highest in the North, especially in Vermont, and lowest in California and the Southwest. Tuition at public two-year colleges is closer to four-year tuition in the northern half of the country. In particular, New York and Utah, with relatively inexpensive four-year tuition, have relatively expensive two-year tuition. The comparative tuition costs between two-year and four-year schools range from 97 percent in New York to 9 percent in California. Megalopolis, the Midwest, and the West pay community college faculties the highest salaries.

Outcomes of Higher Education

The proportion of adults who have college degrees is very high in the Northeast and in the West. In terms of individual states, Massachusetts and California are leaders, with about one in four adults having completed four years of college. In contrast, the South and the Midwest lag behind. The largest proportion of African-Americans with four years of college is found in the West, while Hispanics fare best in the Midwest and South and worst in the West, where they make up a larger proportion of the population.

Attainment of bachelor's, master's, doctor's, and first professional degrees is mapped by state. The general impression of superior achievement in the Northeast and West is confirmed.

Student Costs and Student Aid

Student costs for higher education are highest in the Northeast and on the West Coast. Vermont is the highest-cost state. Private colleges are also costliest in the North and on the West Coast, and least costly in the Great Plains and Southwest. New York has the lowest in-state tuition in the North but is a relatively high-cost state because of room and board. Arizona has extremely expensive room and board costs. On average, New England has the most costly private colleges. Generally, private costs and public costs are either both relatively high or both relatively low. States such as Louisiana with high private costs and low public costs are rare.

New York stands out in state spending for undergraduate aid, providing one-quarter of the national total. Northeastern states, especially Vermont and New York, tend to offset high student costs with grants to students, although grants may be made to students in public or private colleges. In New York, two-thirds of undergraduates received some type of grant. States in the Northeast spend a larger percentage of higher education revenues on student grants; those in the Deep South spend the smallest proportion.

Financing of Higher Education

States that spend the most money per student tend to be in the North rather than the South, and in the East rather than in the West. Economy of scale is at work because states with larger enrollments tend to spend less per student. Northeastern states tend to spend the smallest proportion of their budgets on higher education; those in the West and South the largest proportion. Eastern states, especially those in the Southeast, have had the largest percentage increase in expenditures for higher education in recent years. Federal funding is concentrated in eight states with large populations and large research-oriented institutions. Universities receiving the most federal dollars are in the Northeast and California, and they tend to be either large, prestigious private schools or flagship state institutions. The Northeast, especially southern New England, and the West Coast, especially California, receive the most federal dollars per faculty member. Universities with the largest endowments are mostly private schools concentrated in the Northeast and Midwest. Colleges receiving the most federal funding for research and development are concentrated in the Northeastern quadrant of the country and in California.

Finally, we present two more maps.

10.1 ASSESSMENT

The first is a map of "Assessment" (map 10.1). Assessment is a trend that has swept higher-education institutions over the last few years. Institutions are asked to state their specific educational goals and the achievement of these goals is measured by evaluating outcomes. Unlike traditional program reviews, the focus is on the achievement of the individual learner: What was he or she supposed to learn? How can these learning outcomes best be measured? How well is the institution accomplishing its own goals in educating students?

Assessment has spread rapidly due to the initiatives of state legislative and higher-education authorities. The strongest push for assessment has come from thirteen states where state legislatures have required some type of assessment. Such action often grows out of a concern by politicians and citizens to ensure that they are "getting their money's worth" from the investment in institutions of higher education. These states are concentrated in the Southeast and the Southwest but include a few outliers in Ohio and Hawaii. A few have particularly strong assessment requirements, and their concern may have diffused to other states in their regions. Florida was an early initiator of assessment and gained national attention in 1979 when the state legislature mandated the Florida Board of Education to adopt minimum academic standards in computation and communication for college students. Texas similarly created its Academic Skills Test in 1987 and extended assessment to the doctoral level by requiring five-year reviews of the quality and productivity of all doctoral programs at public institutions.

In other cases, action has been taken by a state council or state board of higher education that has required or coordinated assessment among its member institutions. These nineteen states are scattered mainly across the northern half of the country but also include a few southern states such as Alabama, Louisiana, and Arkansas. The eighteen states without any formal state board or legislative action do not form any particularly geographic pattern except that they tend not to be in the Southeast or Southwest. While these eighteen states have taken no formal action yet, a report on assessment by the Educational Commission of the States estimates that only six states have nothing in place or planned in regard to assessment (Michigan, Oklahoma, North Dakota, Pennsylvania, Vermont, and Wyoming).

10.2 SUMMARY MAP

Another way of summarizing the data mapped in this atlas is to combine several major representative measures of education into a single composite measure, comparable to the various composite indicators used to measure quality of life. We have done this on map 10.2. This index is not intended to be a scientific measure of the "health" of the higher-education systems of the various

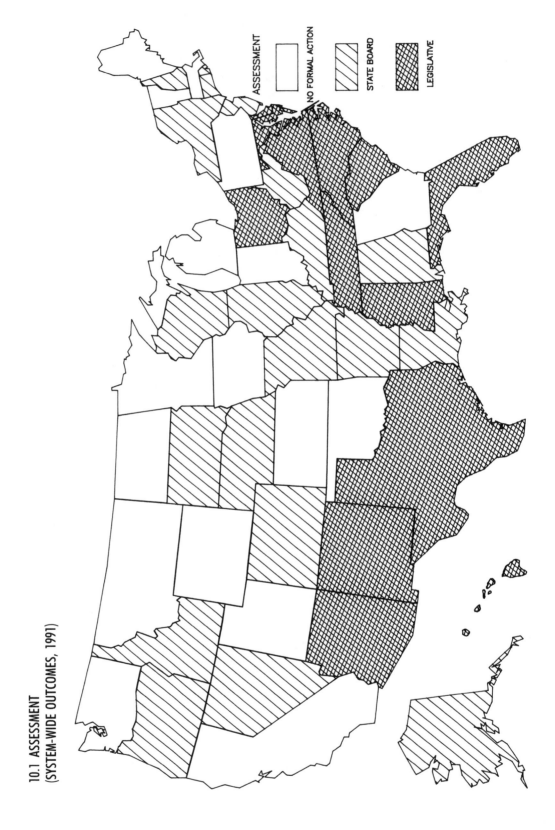

10.1 ASSESSMENT
(SYSTEM-WIDE OUTCOMES, 1991)

ASSESSMENT

NO FORMAL ACTION

STATE BOARD

LEGISLATIVE

10.2 SUMMARY MAP

INDEX

LESS THAN 1.6

1.6 TO 1.9

MORE THAN 1.9

states. It is highly general and impressionistic, but we think it is useful in calling attention to the relative standings among states on a limited number of variables. The reader will note that the measures we have used are biased toward public higher education. This is appropriate, however, given the larger proportion of students in public rather than in private colleges. The index is but one way of making distinctions among the states. We encourage readers to use the maps and statistical tables to experiment and devise other composite rankings based on variables they select as critical. Eleven variables from different sections of the atlas are included in the composite index. The methodology is very simple; each state is assigned a weight of 1, 2, or 3 depending on low, medium, or high standing on the eleven maps. The composite index totals these, then divides by eleven to give an average standing. (In the case of net migration of students, states were divided in binary fashion by being assigned + 1 or − 1.)

One measure we chose from the enrollment section is the FTE enrollment per capita (map 2.2). A high ratio of enrollment per population seems to be the single best indicator of a vibrant higher-education system. In addition, we chose the number of bachelor's degrees awarded per 10,000 population (map 7.7). Arguing that education leading to the bachelor's degree is the basic "bread and butter" outcome of what higher education is all about, we ranked higher those states that had larger numbers of degrees per capita. The per capita measure is important to ensure that relative size of population is not the variable that is being measured. Balancing this measure of undergraduate education is map 2.8, Graduate Enrollment as a Proportion of Total Enrollment. The assumption is that states with larger proportions of graduate students are more likely to have major doctoral-granting institutions, significant research programs, and renowned scholars available to their students. We selected the student-faculty ratio, map 3.16, as an important indication of the educational environment in each state for both undergraduate and graduate students; on this measure, we ranked states with lower ratios more highly. On the assumption that (1) the proportion of out-of-state students is one measure of the "cosmopolitan" collegiate atmosphere of a state, and (2) a state attracting a larger proportion of out-of-state students is doing something right, we used map 3.6, Net Migration of Recent Graduates Entering Four-Year Colleges, as our next indicator. In this case a binary division was used to distinguish among the states. Those with net in-migration were assigned a value of + 1; those with net out-migration were assigned a value of − 1.

Average faculty salary (map 3.14) was selected as a gross measure of a state's willingness to attract talented faculty. It is not the only factor, of course, but it is an important one. Equity, the degree of similarity between salaries for men and women, is an important measure of a state's willingness to have its higher-education system free from discriminatory practices (map 3.15). The expenditures of state and local government per FTE student (map 9.1) provides a critical measure of financial support for higher education, as does map 9.2, the proportion of general expenditures spent on higher education. Finally, the cost of in-state tuition (map 8.3) is an index of the extent to which a state passes the burden of the cost of higher education to the consumer. Obviously, high tuition discourages greater participation by both full- and part-time students. Because of the growing importance of two-year colleges in many states, and because of the differences among states in relative cost of two-year and four-year tuition, we also included two-year tuition costs (map 6.6) as a variable. On these measures a high tuition got a low rating.

When the individual state scores were tallied and averaged, no state came close to a "perfect" score of 2.8 (the maximum composite score of 31, divided by eleven measures); and, fortunately, none came close to the poorest possible score of 0.8. Utah and North Carolina ranked highest at 2.3, followed by Iowa at 2.2, and Arizona, Delaware, and Oregon at 2.1. On the opposite side of the scale, the lowest ranking, 1.4, was received by only two states: Maine and Mississippi. All states scored high on some of the eleven measures and low on others. Rare were cases like Indiana and Washington, which ranked in the medium category on eight of the eleven measures. On the positive side, this seems to imply that states could make significant improvements in overall quality of higher education by targeting a few key sectors for improvement.

The map of the composite index (map 10.2) shows a limited regional pattern. The states in all the categories seem well balanced between East and West, North and South. Among the states of the East Coast, Georgia, North Carolina, Virginia, Delaware form a not-quite contiguous band of states in the highest category. The Northeast, on the other hand, divides between Maine and New Jersey in the lowest category and Massachusetts and Rhode Island in the highest. States in and around the Midwest divide along an east-west line: Michigan, Ohio, Kentucky, and Illinois fall in the lowest category, but Wisconsin, Iowa, and Missouri fall in the highest. Ohio is a real surprise; for all the prestige of Ohio State and the state's many private schools, it falls in the lowest category. West of the Great Plains, Oregon, Wyoming, Utah, Colorado, and Arizona are in the highest category, but neighboring Montana and Nevada are in the lowest. In the South, in addition to the four southern Atlantic Coast states already mentioned, Oklahoma also ranks in the highest category. Neighboring Arkansas and Mississippi, however, fall in the lowest category. Many of the large-population and, in some cases, fast-growing states are in the middle category: California, Texas, New York, and Florida are among this group.

The outcome of the composite index brings us back to our opening theme. The United States is a big country, and our higher-education system is divided into fifty state systems, a condition unique among the urbanized industrialized countries. There is great diversity and variation from state to state on almost all demographic and statistical indicators of higher education. Often, regional patterns emerged on our maps—as in obvious cases such as black and Hispanic proportions, faculty salaries, and student costs. In other cases, the initiative of individual states transcended regional patterns, indicating that states need not be prisoners of regional trends. State patterns are critical, not only from the perspective of the cultural geographer, public policymaker, or educational administrator, but more importantly from the perspective of the individual college-bound student. While in theory the nation offers an incredible variety of educational opportunities for those with the financial means and initiative to exercise these options, the reality is that many students are place-bound by issues of income, accessibility, and family circumstances. For the vast majority of students who attend college in their home states, the relative condition of the higher-educational system in that state is critical. These fifty separate systems of higher education deserve much more discussion and analysis than is readily available. We hope this atlas has made a contribution to that end and that it will inspire further, more detailed research along these lines.

Appendix of Tables

Table 1.1
State Abbreviations

Alabama	AL	Kentucky	KY	North Dakota	ND
Alaska	AK	Louisiana	LA	Ohio	OH
Arizona	AZ	Maine	ME	Oklahoma	OK
Arkansas	AR	Maryland	MD	Oregon	OR
California	CA	Massachusetts	MA	Pennsylvania	PA
Colorado	CO	Michigan	MI	Rhode Island	RI
Connecticut	CT	Minnesota	MN	South Carolina	SC
Delaware	DE	Mississippi	MS	South Dakota	SD
D.C.	DC	Missouri	MO	Tennessee	TN
Florida	FL	Montana	MT	Texas	TX
Georgia	GA	Nebraska	NB	Utah	UT
Hawaii	HI	Nevada	NV	Vermont	VT
Idaho	ID	New Hampshire	NH	Virginia	VA
Illinois	IL	New Jersey	NJ	Washington	WA
Indiana	IN	New Mexico	NM	West Virginia	WV
Iowa	IA	New York	NY	Wisconsin	WI
Kansas	KS	North Carolina	NC	Wyoming	WY

Table 1.2

U.S. Population by State, 1990
(rank in parentheses)

Alabama (22)	3,984,384	Kentucky (23)	3,665,220	North Dakota (47)	634,223
Alaska (50)	545,774	Louisiana (21)	4,180,831	Ohio (7)	10,777,514
Arizona (24)	3,619,064	Maine (38)	1,218,053	Oklahoma (28)	3,123,799
Arkansas (33)	2,337,395	Maryland (19)	4,732,934	Oregon (29)	2,828,214
California (1)	29,279,015	Massachusetts (13)	5,928,331	Pennsylvania (5)	11,764,434
Colorado (26)	3,272,460	Michigan (8)	9,179,661	Rhode Island (43)	988,609
Connecticut (27)	3,226,929	Minnesota (20)	4,358,864	South Carolina (25)	3,407,389
Delaware (46)	658,031	Mississippi (31)	2,534,814	South Dakota (45)	693,294
D.C. (48)	574,844	Missouri (15)	5,079,385	Tennessee (18)	4,822,134
Florida (4)	12,774,603	Montana (44)	794,329	Texas (3)	16,824,665
Georgia (11)	6,386,948	Nebraska (36)	1,572,503	Utah (35)	1,711,117
Hawaii (41)	1,095,237	Nevada (39)	1,193,285	Vermont (49)	560,029
Idaho (42)	1,003,558	New Hampshire (40)	1,103,163	Virginia (12)	6,127,680
Illinois (6)	11,325,247	New Jersey (9)	7,617,418	Washington (17)	4,826,675
Indiana (14)	5,498,725	New Mexico (37)	1,490,381	West Virginia (34)	1,782,958
Iowa (30)	2,766,658	New York (2)	17,626,586	Wisconsin (16)	4,869,640
Kansas (32)	2,467,845	North Carolina (10)	6,552,927	Wyoming (51)	449,905

SOURCE: U.S. Bureau of the Census, 1991.

Table 1.3

Metropolitan Area Population
(percentage of state population, 1990)

Alabama (27)	67.4%	Kentucky (39)	46.5%	North Dakota (42)	40.3%
Alaska (41)	41.1	Louisiana (22)	69.5	Ohio (17)	79.0
Arizona (17)	79.0	Maine (45)	35.9	Oklahoma (33)	59.4
Arkansas (43)	40.1	Maryland (4)	92.8	Oregon (23)	68.5
California (3)	95.7	Massachusetts (9)	90.4	Pennsylvania (10)	84.8
Colorado (15)	81.5	Michigan (16)	80.1	Rhode Island (5)	92.5
Connecticut (6)	92.4	Minnesota (25)	67.7	South Carolina (32)	60.6
Delaware (29)	66.3	Mississippi (46)	30.1	South Dakota (48)	29.5
D.C. (1)	100.0	Missouri (30)	66.2	Tennessee (25)	67.7
Florida (8)	90.8	Montana (49)	23.9	Texas (14)	81.6
Georgia (31)	65.0	Nebraska (37)	48.5	Utah (19)	77.5
Hawaii (20)	75.5	Nevada (11)	82.9	Vermont (50)	23.4
Idaho (51)	20.4	New Hampshire (35)	56.1	Virginia (21)	72.5
Illinois (12)	82.7	New Jersey (1)	100.0	Washington (13)	81.7
Indiana (23)	68.5	New Mexico (38)	48.4	West Virginia (44)	36.4
Iowa (40)	44.0	New York (7)	91.1	Wisconsin (27)	67.4
Kansas (36)	53.8	North Carolina (34)	56.7	Wyoming (47)	29.6

SOURCE: *Statistical Abstract of the United States 1991*, 111th ed. (Washington, D.C.: U.S. Bureau of the Census, 1991), table 35.

Table 1.4

African-American Population
(percent African-American, 1990)

Alabama (6)	25.3%	Kentucky (26)	7.1%	North Dakota (45)	0.6%
Alaska (31)	4.1	Louisiana (3)	30.8	Ohio (20)	10.6
Arizona (37)	3.0	Maine (48)	0.4	Oklahoma (24)	7.4
Arkansas (12)	15.9	Maryland (7)	24.9	Oregon (42)	1.6
California (24)	7.4	Massachusetts (29)	5.0	Pennsylvania (21)	9.2
Colorado (32)	4.0	Michigan (15)	13.9	Rhode Island (33)	3.9
Connecticut (22)	8.3	Minnesota (39)	2.2	South Carolina (4)	29.8
Delaware (10)	16.9	Mississippi (2)	35.6	South Dakota (47)	0.5
D.C. (1)	65.8	Missouri (19)	10.7	Tennessee (11)	16.0
Florida (16)	13.6	Montana (49)	0.3	Texas (18)	11.9
Georgia (5)	27.0	Nebraska (34)	3.6	Utah (44)	0.7
Hawaii (38)	2.5	Nevada (27)	6.6	Vermont (49)	0.3
Idaho (49)	0.3	New Hampshire (45)	0.6	Virginia (9)	18.8
Illinois (14)	14.8	New Jersey (17)	13.4	Washington (35)	3.1
Indiana (23)	7.8	New Mexico (40)	2.0	West Virginia (35)	3.1
Iowa (41)	1.7	New York (12)	15.9	Wisconsin (29)	5.0
Kansas (28)	5.8	North Carolina (8)	22.0	Wyoming (43)	0.8

SOURCE: *1990 Census Profile: Race and Hispanic Origin*, no. 2, June 1991, U.S. Bureau of the Census.

Table 1.5

Hispanic Population
(percent Hispanic, 1990)

Alabama (47)	0.6%	Kentucky (47)	47.6%	North Dakota (44)	44.7%
Alaska (22)	3.2	Louisiana (28)	2.2	Ohio (35)	1.3
Arizona (4)	18.8	Maine (47)	0.6	Oklahoma (23)	2.7
Arkansas (42)	0.8	Maryland (24)	2.6	Oregon (20)	4.0
California (2)	25.8	Massachusetts (17)	4.8	Pennsylvania (30)	2.0
Colorado (5)	12.9	Michigan (28)	2.2	Rhode Island (18)	4.6
Connecticut (12)	6.5	Minnesota (36)	1.2	South Carolina (41)	0.9
Delaware (26)	2.4	Mississippi (47)	0.6	South Dakota (42)	0.8
D.C. (14)	5.4	Missouri (36)	1.2	Tennessee (44)	0.7
Florida (7)	12.2	Montana (34)	1.5	Texas (3)	25.5
Georgia (33)	1.7	Nebraska (27)	2.3	Utah (16)	4.9
Hawaii (11)	7.3	Nevada (8)	10.4	Vermont (44)	0.7
Idaho (15)	5.3	New Hampshire (40)	1.0	Virginia (24)	2.6
Illinois (10)	7.9	New Jersey (9)	9.6	Washington (19)	4.4
Indiana (32)	1.8	New Mexico (1)	38.2	West Virginia (51)	0.5
Iowa (36)	1.2	New York (6)	12.3	Wisconsin (31)	1.9
Kansas (21)	3.8	North Carolina (36)	1.2	Wyoming (13)	5.7

SOURCE: *1990 Census Profile: Race and Hispanic Origin*, no. 2, June 1991, U.S. Bureau of the Census.

Table 1.6
Median Household Income, 1990

Alabama (49)	21,109	Kentucky (43)	23,512	North Dakota (38)	25,075
Alaska (5)	36,029	Louisiana (45)	23,000	Ohio (21)	29,046
Arizona (25)	28,300	Maine (26)	27,863	Oklahoma (40)	24,132
Arkansas (50)	21,101	Maryland (4)	36,396	Oregon (24)	28,365
California (9)	33,002	Massachusetts (6)	36,000	Pennsylvania (23)	28,484
Colorado (28)	26,996	Michigan (15)	30,910	Rhode Island (18)	30,000
Connecticut (1)	42,362	Minnesota (17)	30,134	South Carolina (42)	23,820
Delaware (10)	32,254	Mississippi (51)	19,774	South Dakota (41)	24,086
D.C. (30)	26,350	Missouri (32)	26,155	Tennessee (46)	22,706
Florida (35)	26,000	Montana (44)	23,287	Texas (36)	25,701
Georgia (27)	27,552	Nebraska (33)	26,048	Utah (16)	30,500
Hawaii (7)	35,000	Nevada (19)	29,100	Vermont (12)	31,592
Idaho (39)	24,550	New Hampshire (3)	37,500	Virginia (8)	34,066
Illinois (13)	31,255	New Jersey (2)	39,012	Washington (11)	32,030
Indiana (37)	25,600	New Mexico (47)	22,500	West Virginia (48)	21,535
Iowa (31)	26,168	New York (14)	31,200	Wisconsin (20)	29,050
Kansas (28)	26,800	North Carolina (34)	26,042	Wyoming (22)	29,000

SOURCE: Population Reference Bureau, *The United States Population Data Sheet*, February 1991.

Table 1.7
Oldest Colleges
(founded before 1800)

Harvard University, MA	1636
College of William and Mary, VA	1693
St. John's College, MD	1696
Yale University, CT	1701
University of Pennsylvania, PA	1740
Moravian College, PA	1742
University of Delaware, DE	1743
Princeton University, NJ	1746
Washington and Lee University, VA	1749
Columbia College, NY	1754
Columbia University, School of General Studies, NY	1754
Brown University, RI	1764
Rutgers, The State University of New Jersey, NJ	1766
Dartmouth College, NH	1769
College of Charleston, SC	1770
Salem College, NC	1772
Dickinson College, PA	1773
Hampden-Sydney College, VA	1776
Transylvania University, KY	1780
Washington and Jefferson College, PA	1781
Washington College, MD	1782
Becker Junior College–Leicester Campus, MA	1784

University of Georgia, GA	1785
Castleton State College, VT	1787
Franklin and Marshall College, PA	1787
Louisburg College, NC	1787
University of Pittsburgh, PA	1787
York College of Pennsylvania, PA	1787
Georgetown University, DC	1789
St. Mary's Seminary and University, MD	1791
University of Vermont, VT	1791
Williams College, MA	1793
Bowdoin College, ME	1794
Tusculum College, TN	1794
University of Tennessee, Knoxville, TN	1794
Union College, NY	1795
University of North Carolina at Chapel Hill, NC	1795
Hartwick College, NY	1797
University of Louisville, KY	1798

SOURCE: *Peterson's National College Databank*, 1990, p. 2.

Table 2.1

Total Enrollment
(all institutions of higher education, Fall 1989)

Alabama (22)	208,562	Kentucky (28)	166,014	North Dakota (46)	40,350
Alaska (51)	28,627	Louisiana (24)	179,927	Ohio (8)	550,729
Arizona (19)	252,614	Maine (41)	58,230	Oklahoma (25)	175,855
Arkansas (35)	88,572	Maryland (17)	255,326	Oregon (29)	161,822
California (1)	1,744,879	Massachusetts (9)	426,476	Pennsylvania (5)	610,357
Colorado (23)	201,114	Michigan (7)	560,320	Rhode Island (39)	76,503
Connecticut (27)	169,438	Minnesota (18)	253,097	South Carolina (31)	145,730
Delaware (45)	40,562	Mississippi (32)	116,370	South Dakota (49)	32,666
D.C. (38)	79,800	Missouri (14)	278,505	Tennessee (21)	218,866
Florida (6)	573,712	Montana (47)	37,660	Texas (3)	877,859
Georgia (20)	239,208	Nebraska (34)	108,844	Utah (33)	114,815
Hawaii (43)	54,188	Nevada (42)	56,471	Vermont (48)	35,946
Idaho (44)	48,969	New Hampshire (40)	58,600	Virginia (11)	344,284
Illinois (4)	709,937	New Jersey (12)	314,091	Washington (16)	255,760
Indiana (15)	275,821	New Mexico (37)	81,350	West Virginia (36)	82,455
Iowa (26)	169,901	New York (2)	1,018,130	Wisconsin (13)	290,672
Kansas (30)	158,497	North Carolina (10)	345,401	Wyoming (50)	29,159

SOURCE: *Digest of Education Statistics*, 1991, table 178.

Table 2.2

FTE Enrollment per 1,000 Population, Fall 1989

Alabama (17)	41	Kentucky (42)	34	North Dakota (4)	54
Alaska (42)	34	Louisiana (42)	34	Ohio (31)	38
Arizona (12)	45	Maine (42)	34	Oklahoma (21)	40
Arkansas (47)	30	Maryland (36)	36	Oregon (17)	41
California (31)	38	Massachusetts (3)	55	Pennsylvania (21)	40
Colorado (12)	45	Michigan (17)	41	Rhode Island (2)	58
Connecticut (36)	36	Minnesota (14)	44	South Carolina (46)	33
Delaware (9)	46	Mississippi (31)	38	South Dakota (31)	38
D.C. (1)	103	Missouri (25)	39	Tennessee (39)	35
Florida (47)	30	Montana (25)	39	Texas (36)	36
Georgia (49)	29	Nebraska (7)	49	Utah (5)	52
Hawaii (39)	35	Nevada (50)	28	Vermont (6)	51
Idaho (25)	39	New Hampshire (25)	39	Virginia (21)	40
Illinois (17)	41	New Jersey (50)	28	Washington (25)	39
Indiana (25)	39	New Mexico (31)	38	West Virginia (39)	35
Iowa (7)	49	New York (16)	43	Wisconsin (9)	46
Kansas (9)	46	North Carolina (21)	40	Wyoming (14)	44

SOURCE: Calculated from table 190, *Digest of Education Statistics, 1991*, and 1989 population estimates, U.S. Bureau of the Census.

Table 2.3

Enrollment Growth
(percent change, Fall 1980 to Fall 1989)

Alabama (8)	27%	Kentucky (23)	16%	North Dakota (21)	18%
Alaska (6)	34	Louisiana (32)	12	Ohio (30)	13
Arizona (9)	25	Maine (5)	35	Oklahoma (34)	10
Arkansas (26)	14	Maryland (30)	13	Oregon (44)	3
California (49)	−3	Massachusetts (46)	2	Pennsylvania (34)	10
Colorado (12)	23	Michigan (38)	8	Rhode Island (26)	14
Connecticut (43)	6	Minnesota (15)	22	South Carolina (34)	10
Delaware (12)	23	Mississippi (26)	14	South Dakota (47)	0
D.C. (50)	−8	Missouri (20)	19	Tennessee (41)	7
Florida (3)	39	Montana (41)	7	Texas (9)	25
Georgia (7)	30	Nebraska (15)	22	Utah (15)	22
Hawaii (25)	15	Nevada (1)	40	Vermont (22)	17
Idaho (26)	14	New Hampshire (9)	25	Virginia (12)	23
Illinois (34)	10	New Jersey (48)	−2	Washington (51)	−16
Indiana (32)	12	New Mexico (1)	40	West Virginia (38)	8
Iowa (18)	21	New York (44)	3	Wisconsin (38)	8
Kansas (23)	16	North Carolina (19)	20	Wyoming (4)	38

SOURCE: Calculated from table 178, *Digest of Education Statistics, 1991*.

Table 2.4
Enrollment in Public Colleges, Fall 1989

Alabama (20)	187,575	Kentucky (28)	138.297	North Dakota (43)	37,501
Alaska (48)	26,274	Louisiana (24)	151,733	Ohio (7)	412,073
Arizona (13)	239,314	Maine (41)	40,511	Oklahoma (25)	151,410
Arkansas (36)	76,416	Maryland (15)	217,562	Oregon (27)	141,311
California (1)	1,534,209	Massachusetts (19)	187,772	Pennsylvania (8)	335,101
Colorado (22)	175,850	Michigan (6)	479,714	Rhode Island (40)	40,604
Connecticut (31)	109,697	Minnesota (17)	198,610	South Carolina (29)	118,639
Delaware (45)	33,037	Mississippi (32)	103,035	South Dakota (49)	25,075
D.C. (51)	12,439	Missouri (18)	192,322	Tennessee (23)	167,056
Florida (5)	480,869	Montana (44)	33,197	Texas (2)	782,495
Georgia (21)	186,776	Nebraska (33)	91,337	Utah (34)	79,623
Hawaii (39)	43,644	Nevada (38)	56,184	Vermont (50)	20,925
Idaho (42)	38,447	New Hampshire (46)	32,889	Virginia (9)	287,624
Illinois (4)	536,643	New Jersey (11)	253,544	Washington (14)	221,362
Indiana (16)	216,433	New Mexico (35)	79,359	West Virginia (37)	72,478
Iowa (30)	116,889	New York (3)	600,587	Wisconsin (12)	245,968
Kansas (26)	145,134	North Carolina (10)	277,062	Wyoming (47)	28,553

SOURCE: *Digest of Education Statistics*, 1991, table 179.

Table 2.5
Enrollment in Private Colleges, Fall 1989

Alabama (32)	20,987	Kentucky (26)	28,717	North Dakota (47)	2,849
Alaska (48)	2,353	Louisiana (27)	28,194	Ohio (6)	138,656
Arizona (39)	13,300	Maine (34)	17,719	Oklahoma (31)	24,445
Arkansas (40)	12,156	Maryland (22)	37,764	Oregon (33)	20,511
California (4)	210,670	Massachusetts (3)	238,704	Pennsylvania (2)	275,256
Colorado (30)	25,264	Michigan (10)	80,606	Rhode Island (23)	35,899
Connecticut (14)	59,741	Minnesota (17)	54,487	South Carolina (28)	27,091
Delaware (45)	7,525	Mississippi (38)	13,335	South Dakota (44)	7,591
D.C. (12)	67,361	Missouri (9)	86,183	Tennessee (20)	51,810
Florida (8)	92,843	Montana (46)	4,463	Texas (7)	95,364
Georgia (19)	52,432	Nebraska (35)	17,507	Utah (24)	35,192
Hawaii (41)	10,544	Nevada (51)	287	Vermont (36)	15,021
Idaho (42)	10,522	New Hampshire (29)	25,711	Virginia (16)	56,660
Illinois (5)	173,294	New Jersey (13)	60,547	Washington (25)	34,398
Indiana (15)	59,388	New Mexico (49)	1,991	West Virginia (43)	9,977
Iowa (18)	53,012	New York (1)	417,543	Wisconsin (21)	44,704
Kansas (37)	13,363	North Carolina (11)	68,339	Wyoming (50)	606

SOURCE: *Digest of Education Statistics*, 1991, table 180.

Table 2.6

Proportion of Enrollment in Private Four-Year Colleges, Fall 1989

Alabama (39)	13%	Kentucky (32)	18%	North Dakota (44)	8%
Alaska (45)	7	Louisiana (34)	16	Ohio (20)	28
Arizona (41)	11	Maine (14)	32	Oklahoma (34)	16
Arkansas (38)	14	Maryland (23)	25	Oregon (27)	23
California (19)	29	Massachusetts (2)	67	Pennsylvania (6)	48
Colorado (34)	16	Michigan (27)	23	Rhode Island (3)	59
Connecticut (7)	47	Minnesota (21)	27	South Carolina (28)	22
Delaware (23)	25	Mississippi (37)	15	South Dakota (28)	22
D.C. (1)	84	Missouri (11)	41	Tennessee (16)	30
Florida (13)	34	Montana (42)	10	Texas (32)	18
Georgia (25)	24	Nebraska (28)	22	Utah (12)	39
Hawaii (15)	31	Nevada (48)	1	Vermont (9)	44
Idaho (45)	7	New Hampshire (5)	50	Virginia (22)	26
Illinois (8)	46	New Jersey (16)	30	Washington (19)	29
Indiana (25)	24	New Mexico (47)	4	West Virginia (42)	10
Iowa (10)	43	New York (4)	52	Wisconsin (28)	22
Kansas (40)	12	North Carolina (16)	30	Wyoming	Not applicable

SOURCE: Calculated from table 189, *Digest of Education Statistics, 1991*.

Table 2.7

Graduate and First Professional Enrollment, Fall 1989

Alabama (26)	22,970	Kentucky (30)	20,699	North Dakota (47)	4,016
Alaska (51)	1,109	Louisiana (24)	25,551	Ohio (7)	72,031
Arizona (23)	26,494	Maine (43)	4,955	Oklahoma (25)	24,312
Arkansas (40)	7,610	Maryland (13)	39,208	Oregon (32)	18,729
California (1)	198,192	Massachusetts (6)	84,913	Pennsylvania (5)	86,977
Colorado (27)	22,434	Michigan (8)	67,410	Rhode Island (38)	9,583
Connecticut (17)	35,084	Minnesota (18)	30,245	South Carolina (31)	20,323
Delaware (45)	4,805	Mississippi (34)	12,018	South Dakota (48)	3,815
D.C. (19)	30,189	Missouri (12)	41,763	Tennessee (22)	26,545
Florida (9)	58,152	Montana (49)	3,652	Texas (3)	110,996
Georgia (15)	36,415	Nebraska (33)	13,655	Utah (36)	10,421
Hawaii (41)	6,827	Nevada (44)	4,861	Vermont (46)	4,436
Idaho (42)	6,480	New Hampshire (39)	7,886	Virginia (11)	46,915
Illinois (4)	102,663	New Jersey (10)	47,215	Washington (29)	20,786
Indiana (16)	36,264	New Mexico (35)	10,925	West Virginia (37)	10,340
Iowa (21)	26,965	New York (2)	189,786	Wisconsin (20)	29,052
Kansas (28)	21,333	North Carolina (14)	37,421	Wyoming (50)	3,011

SOURCE: *Digest of Education Statistics, 1991*, table 185.

Table 2.8
Graduate Enrollment as a Proportion of Total Enrollment, Fall 1989

Alabama (35)	11%	Kentucky (26)	12%	North Dakota (39)	10%
Alaska (51)	4	Louisiana (10)	14	Ohio (16)	13
Arizona (39)	10	Maine (46)	9	Oklahoma (10)	14
Arkansas (46)	9	Maryland (6)	15	Oregon (26)	12
California (35)	11	Massachusetts (3)	20	Pennsylvania (10)	14
Colorado (35)	11	Michigan (26)	12	Rhode Island (26)	12
Connecticut (2)	21	Minnesota (26)	12	South Carolina (10)	14
Delaware (26)	12	Mississippi (39)	10	South Dakota (26)	12
D.C. (1)	38	Missouri (6)	15	Tennessee (26)	12
Florida (39)	10	Montana (39)	10	Texas (16)	13
Georgia (6)	15	Nebraska (16)	13	Utah (46)	9
Hawaii (16)	13	Nevada (46)	9	Vermont (26)	12
Idaho (16)	13	New Hampshire (16)	13	Virginia (10)	14
Illinois (10)	14	New Jersey (6)	15	Washington (50)	8
Indiana (16)	13	New Mexico (16)	13	West Virginia (16)	13
Iowa (5)	16	New York (4)	19	Wisconsin (39)	10
Kansas (16)	13	North Carolina (35)	11	Wyoming (39)	10

SOURCE: Calculated from tables 178 and 185, *Digest of Education Statistics, 1991.*

Table 2.9
Private Graduate Enrollment as a Proportion of Total Graduate Enrollment, Fall 1989

Alabama (42)	9%	Kentucky (36)	14%	North Dakota (45)	4%
Alaska (34)	15	Louisiana (24)	28	Ohio (24)	28
Arizona (36)	14	Maine (26)	26	Oklahoma (33)	16
Arkansas (47)	3	Maryland (14)	38	Oregon (26)	26
California (10)	47	Massachusetts (2)	77	Pennsylvania (6)	54
Colorado (19)	31	Michigan (34)	15	Rhode Island (12)	42
Connecticut (8)	53	Minnesota (18)	35	South Carolina (40)	10
Delaware (11)	43	Mississippi (32)	17	South Dakota (43)	8
D.C. (1)	97	Missouri (8)	53	Tennessee (23)	29
Florida (15)	37	Montana (47)	3	Texas (30)	19
Georgia (20)	30	Nebraska (36)	14	Utah (20)	30
Hawaii (39)	12	Nevada	Not applicable	Vermont (6)	54
Idaho (40)	10	New Hampshire (3)	66	Virginia (31)	18
Illinois (5)	55	New Jersey (15)	37	Washington (15)	37
Indiana (29)	21	New Mexico (49)	1	West Virginia (44)	6
Iowa (12)	42	New York (4)	65	Wisconsin (28)	23
Kansas (45)	4	North Carolina (20)	30	Wyoming	Not applicable

SOURCE: Calculated from tables 185 and 186, *Digest of Education Statistics, 1991.*

Table 2.10

Part-Time Students as a Proportion of Total Enrollment, Fall 1989

Alabama (43)	31%	Kentucky (33)	36%	North Dakota (51)	20%
Alaska (2)	63	Louisiana (47)	28	Ohio (25)	40
Arizona (3)	57	Maine (11)	46	Oklahoma (18)	43
Arkansas (46)	29	Maryland (5)	54	Oregon (15)	44
California (4)	56	Massachusetts (29)	38	Pennsylvania (35)	35
Colorado (24)	41	Michigan (10)	49	Rhode Island (27)	39
Connecticut (7)	50	Minnesota (25)	40	South Carolina (40)	32
Delaware (27)	39	Mississippi (50)	24	South Dakota (47)	28
D.C. (31)	37	Missouri (18)	43	Tennessee (38)	34
Florida (6)	53	Montana (49)	26	Texas (11)	46
Georgia (38)	34	Nebraska (15)	44	Utah (35)	35
Hawaii (18)	43	Nevada (1)	69	Vermont (40)	32
Idaho (43)	31	New Hampshire (22)	42	Virginia (13)	45
Illinois (7)	50	New Jersey (7)	50	Washington (22)	42
Indiana (35)	35	New Mexico (13)	45	West Virginia (40)	32
Iowa (45)	30	New York (29)	38	Wisconsin (33)	36
Kansas (18)	43	North Carolina (31)	37	Wyoming (15)	44

SOURCE: Calculated from table 181, *Digest of Education Statistics, 1991.*

Table 2.11

Full-Time Enrollment Majority: Male or Female? Fall 1989

Alabama (6)	F	9,952	Kentucky (10)	F	8,749	North Dakota (48)	M	1,933
Alaska (32)	F	844	Louisiana (8)	F	9,320	Ohio (9)	F	8,973
Arizona (51)	M	4,607	Maine (29)	F	1,112	Oklahoma (45)	M	728
Arkansas (16)	F	5,463	Maryland (21)	F	4,583	Oregon (41)	M	157
California (7)	F	9,379	Massachusetts (4)	F	13,504	Pennsylvania (18)	F	4,934
Colorado (46)	M	821	Michigan (5)	F	10,878	Rhode Island (33)	F	818
Connecticut (24)	F	3,010	Minnesota (19)	F	4,781	South Carolina (14)	F	5,757
Delaware (25)	F	2,646	Mississippi (11)	F	7,477	South Dakota (34)	F	741
D.C. (23)	F	3,854	Missouri (26)	F	2,352	Tennessee (12)	F	7,089
Florida (20)	F	4,757	Montana (37)	F	383	Texas (27)	F	2,179
Georgia (15)	F	5,489	Nebraska (39)	F	315	Utah (50)	M	3,514
Hawaii (28)	F	1,390	Nevada (38)	F	324	Vermont (35)	F	726
Idaho (31)	F	871	New Hampshire (42)	M	235	Virginia (3)	F	13,560
Illinois (40)	F	56	New Jersey (22)	F	4,323	Washington (17)	F	4,951
Indiana (43)	M	273	New Mexico (36)	F	554	West Virginia (30)	F	985
Iowa (49)	M	2,616	New York (1)	F	31,074	Wisconsin (13)	F	6,738
Kansas (47)	M	1,496	North Carolina (2)	F	17,351	Wyoming (44)	M	585

SOURCE: Calculated from table 181, *Digest of Education Statistics, 1991.*
NOTE: M or F indicates which gender is in the majority; the number indicates the amount of the majority. Ranking is by amount of female majority.

Table 2.12
Women Enrolled Full-Time as a Proportion of Total Enrollment, Fall 1989

Alabama (5)	37%	Kentucky (9)	35%	North Dakota (4)	38%
Alaska (50)	20	Louisiana (2)	39	Ohio (24)	31
Arizona (49)	21	Maine (34)	28	Oklahoma (34)	28
Arkansas (2)	39	Maryland (46)	24	Oregon (34)	28
California (48)	22	Massachusetts (19)	33	Pennsylvania (19)	33
Colorado (31)	29	Michigan (42)	26	Rhode Island (24)	31
Connecticut (42)	26	Minnesota (24)	31	South Carolina (8)	36
Delaware (12)	34	Mississippi (1)	41	South Dakota (5)	37
D.C. (12)	34	Missouri (31)	29	Tennessee (12)	34
Florida (46)	24	Montana (5)	37	Texas (40)	27
Georgia (12)	34	Nebraska (34)	28	Utah (24)	31
Hawaii (28)	30	Nevada (51)	16	Vermont (9)	35
Idaho (9)	35	New Hampshire (31)	29	Virginia (28)	30
Illinois (45)	25	New Jersey (42)	26	Washington (28)	30
Indiana (22)	32	New Mexico (34)	28	West Virginia (12)	34
Iowa (12)	34	New York (22)	32	Wisconsin (19)	33
Kansas (34)	28	North Carolina (12)	34	Wyoming (40)	27

SOURCE: Calculated from table 181, *Digest of Education Statistics, 1991*.

Table 2.13
Average Enrollment at Public Four-Year Colleges, Fall 1989

Alabama (39)	6,731	Kentucky (12)	12,792	North Dakota (46)	4,953
Alaska (27)	8,758	Louisiana (23)	9,561	Ohio (17)	11,374
Arizona (1)	32,092	Maine (49)	4,279	Oklahoma (38)	6,763
Arkansas (43)	5,866	Maryland (35)	7,869	Oregon (30)	8,347
California (6)	15,939	Massachusetts (33)	8,016	Pennsylvania (44)	5,460
Colorado (32)	8,256	Michigan (3)	17,037	Rhode Island (13)	12,602
Connecticut (24)	9,347	Minnesota (9)	13,490	South Carolina (40)	6,604
Delaware (16)	11,540	Mississippi (41)	6,302	South Dakota (51)	3,582
D.C. (42)	6,220	Missouri (25)	9,311	Tennessee (19)	10,778
Florida (4)	16,858	Montana (48)	4,744	Texas (21)	10,260
Georgia (37)	7,170	Nebraska (29)	8,460	Utah (7)	13,611
Hawaii (36)	7,704	Nevada (8)	13,543	Vermont (50)	4,032
Idaho (31)	8,273	New Hampshire (47)	4,938	Virginia (20)	10,551
Illinois (5)	16,243	New Jersey (22)	9,650	Washington (10)	13,065
Indiana (11)	12,949	New Mexico (34)	7,932	West Virginia (45)	5,186
Iowa (2)	22,740	New York (28)	8,537	Wisconsin (15)	11,627
Kansas (18)	11,148	North Carolina (26)	9,026	Wyoming (14)	12,335

SOURCE: Calculated from tables 184 and 226, *Digest of Education Statistics, 1991*.

Table 3.1

College Students per 1,000 Population, 1990

Alabama (16)	61.2	Kentucky (40)	48.3	North Dakota (18)	59.3
Alaska (27)	54.2	Louisiana (47)	44.2	Ohio (35)	51.2
Arizona (3)	72.2	Maine (43)	46.6	Oklahoma (26)	55.1
Arkansas (51)	38.5	Maryland (25)	55.4	Oregon (19)	58.6
California (17)	59.5	Massachusetts (7)	69.6	Pennsylvania (37)	50.8
Colorado (6)	70.3	Michigan (14)	61.3	Rhode Island (2)	78.0
Connecticut (32)	51.6	Minnesota (20)	58.0	South Carolina (45)	45.7
Delaware (12)	63.1	Mississippi (41)	47.8	South Dakota (38)	49.1
D.C. (1)	132.9	Missouri (23)	56.6	Tennessee (44)	46.4
Florida (49)	41.6	Montana (46)	44.9	Texas (30)	53.1
Georgia (50)	38.9	Nebraska (4)	71.5	Utah (5)	70.4
Hawaii (39)	48.5	Nevada (34)	51.4	Vermont (10)	64.7
Idaho (33)	51.5	New Hampshire (29)	53.6	Virginia (22)	57.1
Illinois (11)	63.8	New Jersey (48)	41.9	Washington (28)	54.1
Indiana (36)	51.0	New Mexico (24)	56.5	West Virginia (42)	47.3
Iowa (13)	61.4	New York (21)	57.8	Wisconsin (14)	61.3
Kansas (9)	66.0	North Carolina (30)	53.1	Wyoming (8)	69.1

SOURCE: Calculated from table 6 in *Trends in Racial/Ethnic Enrollment in Higher Education, Fall 1980 through Fall 1990,* NECS, Fall 1992, and from 1990 population figures, U.S. Bureau of the Census.

Table 3.2

Sex Ratio of Entering Freshmen
(number of males per 100 females, Fall 1988)

Alabama (40)	85.2	Kentucky (47)	78.3	North Dakota (3)	116.0
Alaska (30)	87.8	Louisiana (48)	75.9	Ohio (22)	92.1
Arizona (1)	122.5	Maine (18)	94.6	Oklahoma (25)	91.1
Arkansas (45)	79.8	Maryland (39)	85.2	Oregon (12)	96.7
California (16)	94.9	Massachusetts (46)	79.2	Pennsylvania (17)	94.7
Colorado (5)	105.8	Michigan (38)	85.3	Rhode Island (10)	97.6
Connecticut (26)	91.0	Minnesota (24)	91.6	South Carolina (42)	82.4
Delaware (50)	73.8	Mississippi (49)	75.1	South Dakota (37)	86.0
D.C. (51)	69.4	Missouri (35)	86.4	Tennessee (33)	86.9
Florida (22)	92.1	Montana (28)	89.8	Texas (15)	95.1
Georgia (31)	87.7	Nebraska (20)	92.6	Utah (29)	89.7
Hawaii (43)	80.9	Nevada (13)	96.5	Vermont (6)	103.7
Idaho (34)	86.6	New Hampshire (21)	92.5	Virginia (44)	80.8
Illinois (11)	96.8	New Jersey (32)	87.2	Washington (14)	95.6
Indiana (19)	94.2	New Mexico (7)	101.8	West Virginia (9)	98.6
Iowa (8)	99.7	New York (36)	86.2	Wisconsin (27)	90.1
Kansas (4)	106.9	North Carolina (41)	85.1	Wyoming (2)	120.8

SOURCE: Calculated from table 166, *Digest of Educational Statistics, 1990.*

Table 3.3
Proportion of In-State Freshmen, Fall 1988

Alabama (28)	79%	Kentucky (7)	88%	North Dakota (39)	71%
Alaska (31)	78	Louisiana (19)	83	Ohio (11)	86
Arizona (9)	87	Maine (39)	71	Oklahoma (3)	91
Arkansas (15)	85	Maryland (19)	83	Oregon (22)	82
California (4)	90	Massachusetts (42)	68	Pennsylvania (35)	77
Colorado (31)	78	Michigan (15)	85	Rhode Island (49)	44
Connecticut (31)	78	Minnesota (25)	80	South Carolina (25)	80
Delaware (47)	57	Mississippi (9)	87	South Dakota (38)	72
D.C. (51)	18	Missouri (28)	79	Tennessee (28)	79
Florida (31)	78	Montana (11)	86	Texas (1)	92
Georgia (25)	80	Nebraska (11)	86	Utah (44)	64
Hawaii (7)	88	Nevada (5)	89	Vermont (50)	43
Idaho (46)	59	New Hampshire (48)	49	Virginia (42)	68
Illinois (1)	92	New Jersey (11)	86	Washington (5)	89
Indiana (37)	75	New Mexico (17)	84	West Virginia (39)	71
Iowa (19)	83	New York (44)	64	Wisconsin (17)	84
Kansas (22)	82	North Carolina (24)	81	Wyoming (35)	77

SOURCE: *Digest of Education Statistics, 1991*, table 193.

Table 3.4
Out-Migration of Recent Graduates Entering Four-Year Colleges, Fall 1988

Alabama (31)	1,753	Kentucky (27)	1,924	North Dakota (49)	469
Alaska (44)	978	Louisiana (26)	1,925	Ohio (8)	8,272
Arizona (37)	1,267	Maine (28)	1,858	Oklahoma (32)	1,617
Arkansas (40)	1,224	Maryland (7)	8,381	Oregon (30)	1,758
California (9)	7,775	Massachusetts (6)	8,526	Pennsylvania (4)	11,519
Colorado (19)	3,615	Michigan (15)	5,291	Rhode Island (33)	1,613
Connecticut (5)	8,881	Minnesota (12)	6,394	South Carolina (23)	2,259
Delaware (42)	1,128	Mississippi (35)	1,408	South Dakota (45)	974
D.C. (41)	1,164	Missouri (17)	3,767	Tennessee (18)	3,673
Florida (10)	7,701	Montana (46)	875	Texas (13)	5,730
Georgia (14)	5,292	Nebraska (29)	1,768	Utah (51)	374
Hawaii (36)	1,301	Nevada (48)	612	Vermont (43)	1,030
Idaho (47)	857	New Hampshire (25)	2,055	Virginia (11)	6,927
Illinois (3)	15,108	New Jersey (1)	20,671	Washington (22)	2,697
Indiana (20)	3,048	New Mexico (39)	1,253	West Virginia (38)	1,260
Iowa (21)	3,031	New York (2)	20,130	Wisconsin (16)	4,292
Kansas (34)	1,604	North Carolina (24)	2,234	Wyoming (50)	429

SOURCE: *Digest of Education Statistics, 1991*, table 193.

Table 3.5

In-Migration of Recent Graduates Entering Four-Year Colleges, Fall 1988

Alabama (13)	5,209	Kentucky (27)	3,482	North Dakota (36)	1,865
Alaska (51)	51	Louisiana (25)	3,708	Ohio (7)	8,495
Arizona (31)	2,575	Maine (42)	1,066	Oklahoma (38)	1,764
Arkansas (35)	1,990	Maryland (22)	3,962	Oregon (32)	2,518
California (16)	4,998	Massachusetts (1)	16,457	Pennsylvania (2)	15,718
Colorado (14)	5,131	Michigan (29)	2,894	Rhode Island (33)	2,163
Connecticut (17)	4,696	Minnesota (15)	5,034	South Carolina (26)	3,634
Delaware (28)	3,096	Mississippi (41)	1,185	South Dakota (43)	1,057
D.C. (18)	4,656	Missouri (21)	4,502	Tennessee (12)	5,314
Florida (8)	6,822	Montana (49)	336	Texas (20)	4,568
Georgia (11)	5,350	Nebraska (40)	1,630	Utah (45)	671
Hawaii (50)	332	Nevada (46)	568	Vermont (34)	2,159
Idaho (47)	561	New Hampshire (23)	3,924	Virginia (6)	8,562
Illinois (10)	5,391	New Jersey (39)	1,727	Washington (37)	1,797
Indiana (4)	9,566	New Mexico (44)	846	West Virginia (24)	3,820
Iowa (19)	4,646	New York (3)	12,227	Wisconsin (9)	6,534
Kansas (30)	2,619	North Carolina (5)	8,991	Wyoming (48)	462

SOURCE: *Digest of Education Statistics, 1991*, table 193.

Table 3.6

Net Migration of Recent Graduates Entering Four-Year Colleges, 1988

Alabama	3.456	Kentucky	1,558	North Dakota	1,396
Alaska	−927	Louisiana	1,783	Ohio	223
Arizona	1,308	Maine	−792	Oklahoma	147
Arkansas	766	Maryland	−4,419	Oregon	760
California	−2,777	Massachusetts	7,931	Pennsylvania	4,199
Colorado	1,516	Michigan	−2,397	Rhode Island	550
Connecticut	−4,185	Minnesota	−1,360	South Carolina	1,375
Delaware	1,968	Mississippi	−223	South Dakota	83
D.C.	3,492	Missouri	735	Tennessee	1,641
Florida	−879	Montana	−539	Texas	−1,162
Georgia	58	Nebraska	−138	Utah	297
Hawaii	−969	Nevada	−44	Vermont	1,129
Idaho	−296	New Hampshire	1,869	Virginia	1,635
Illinois	−9,717	New Jersey	−18,944	Washington	−900
Indiana	6,518	New Mexico	−407	West Virginia	2,560
Iowa	1,615	New York	−7,903	Wisconsin	2,242
Kansas	1,015	North Carolina	6,757	Wyoming	33

SOURCE: *Digest of Education Statistics, 1991*, table 193.

Table 3.7

Number of Foreign Students by State, 1990

Alabama (30)	4,806	Kentucky (33)	2,705	North Dakota (41)	1,352
Alaska (51)	373	Louisiana (28)	5,040	Ohio (8)	14,798

Arizona (19)	6,824	Maine (45)	1,047	Oklahoma (20)	6,297
Arkansas (38)	1,708	Maryland (13)	7,865	Oregon (23)	6,192
California (1)	55,168	Massachusetts (4)	22,320	Pennsylvania (7)	17,571
Colorado (26)	5,287	Michigan (9)	14,366	Rhode Island (37)	1,883
Connecticut (29)	4,979	Minnesota (25)	5,882	South Carolina (34)	2,620
Delaware (44)	1,067	Mississippi (36)	2,094	South Dakota (48)	776
D.C. (11)	9,709	Missouri (16)	7,349	Tennessee (32)	4,317
Florida (5)	20,700	Montana (49)	774	Texas (3)	26,205
Georgia (22)	6,319	Nebraska (35)	2,232	Utah (27)	5,040
Hawaii (31)	4,770	Nevada (46)	964	Vermont (47)	847
Idaho (43)	1,225	New Hampshire (42)	1,323	Virginia (15)	7,487
Illinois (6)	17,771	New Jersey (10)	9,889	Washington (14)	7,625
Indiana (12)	8,061	New Mexico (40)	1,460	West Virginia (39)	1,653
Iowa (17)	7,079	New York (2)	40,558	Wisconsin (18)	6,881
Kansas (21)	6,335	North Carolina (24)	5,911	Wyoming (50)	549

SOURCE: *Open Doors 1990–1991*, Institute of International Education, table 5-5.

Table 3.8

Colleges with the Largest Enrollment of Merit Scholars, 1991

| | | Number of Scholars | | |
| | | | Sponsored by | Map |
Rank	College	Total	the College	Location Number
1	Harvard/Radcliffe	292	0	1
2	Rice University	246	162	2
3	University of Texas, Austin	210	163	3
4	Stanford University	159	0	4
5	Texas A&M University	154	118	5
6	Yale University	144	0	6
7	Princeton University	107	0	7
8	Northwestern University	105	71	8
9	Ohio State University	102	74	9
10	Brigham Young University	100	74	10
10	Duke University	100	10	11
10	Massachusetts Institute of Technology	100	0	12
11	University of Chicago	96	72	13
11	University of Florida	96	79	14
12	University of California at Los Angeles	90	70	15
12	Georgia Institute of Technology	90	72	16
13	Carleton College	86	64	17
14	University of New Orleans	75	63	18
15	Virginia Polytechnic Institute	74	61	19
16	University of Oklahoma	73	53	20
17	University of Houston	70	61	21
18	Cornell University	67	0	22
18	Michigan State University	67	52	23
19	Brown University	60	0	24
20	University of California at Berkeley	58	0	25

SOURCE: National Merit Scholarship Corporation, Annual Report 1991, pp. 17–19.

Table 3.9

Bachelor's Degrees Conferred in Business
(proportion of degrees conferred, 1987)

Alabama (11)	28.1%	Kentucky (26)	24.2%	North Dakota (47)	18.6%
Alaska (33)	23.2	Louisiana (23)	25.3	Ohio (16)	27.0
Arizona (17)	26.9	Maine (51)	14.8	Oklahoma (14)	27.3
Arkansas (17)	26.9	Maryland (43)	20.6	Oregon (43)	20.6
California (37)	21.5	Massachusetts (39)	21.4	Pennsylvania (22)	25.4
Colorado (21)	26.2	Michigan (27)	24.0	Rhode Island (10)	28.4
Connecticut (25)	24.6	Minnesota (37)	21.5	South Carolina (7)	28.8
Delaware (4)	29.3	Mississippi (2)	30.0	South Dakota (48)	17.2
D.C. (42)	21.0	Missouri (12)	27.7	Tennessee (15)	27.1
Florida (6)	29.0	Montana (43)	20.6	Texas (4)	29.3
Georgia (8)	28.5	Nebraska (20)	26.6	Utah (49)	16.6
Hawaii (3)	29.8	Nevada (1)	38.4	Vermont (50)	16.2
Idaho (29)	23.8	New Hampshire (8)	28.5	Virginia (31)	23.4
Illinois (41)	21.3	New Jersey (12)	27.7	Washington (39)	21.4
Indiana (31)	23.4	New Mexico (35)	22.3	West Virginia (24)	25.0
Iowa (17)	26.9	New York (35)	22.3	Wisconsin (34)	23.0
Kansas (28)	23.9	North Carolina (30)	23.7	Wyoming (46)	19.8

SOURCE: Compiled from state tables in *State Higher Education Profiles*, National Center for Education Statistics, 1988.

Table 3.10

Bachelor's Degrees Conferred in Education
(proportion of degrees conferred, 1987)

Alabama (14)	13.0%	Kentucky (13)	13.4%	North Dakota (6)	16.9%
Alaska (9)	15.4	Louisiana (21)	12.0	Ohio (28)	10.4
Arizona (29)	9.9	Maine (30)	9.5	Oklahoma (3)	18.0
Arkansas (2)	20.2	Maryland (43)	5.7	Oregon (19)	12.2
California (50)	2.6	Massachusetts (47)	4.6	Pennsylvania (35)	8.5
Colorado (44)	5.5	Michigan (41)	6.6	Rhode Island (49)	4.3
Connecticut (46)	5.0	Minnesota (19)	12.2	South Carolina (23)	11.4
Delaware (37)	8.0	Mississippi (11)	15.1	South Dakota (5)	17.2
D.C. (51)	2.3	Missouri (17)	12.5	Tennessee (24)	11.0
Florida (33)	8.8	Montana (10)	15.3	Texas (16)	12.7
Georgia (25)	10.9	Nebraska (8)	16.5	Utah (11)	15.1
Hawaii (38)	7.5	Nevada (25)	10.9	Vermont (40)	7.1
Idaho (7)	16.8	New Hampshire (48)	4.4	Virginia (38)	7.5
Illinois (31)	9.3	New Jersey (42)	5.8	Washington (36)	8.3
Indiana (34)	8.7	New Mexico (15)	12.9	West Virginia (4)	17.4
Iowa (18)	12.3	New York (45)	5.1	Wisconsin (27)	10.6
Kansas (22)	11.8	North Carolina (31)	9.3	Wyoming (1)	26.8

SOURCE: Compiled from state tables in *State Higher Education Profiles*, National Center for Education Statistics, 1988.

Table 3.11

Bachelor's Degrees Conferred in Agriculture
(proportion of degrees conferred, 1987)

Alabama (39)	1.5%	Kentucky (13)	3.4%	North Dakota (4)	4.4%
Alaska (7)	3.8	Louisiana (37)	1.7	Ohio (43)	1.2
Arizona (31)	2.0	Maine (9)	3.7	Oklahoma (18)	2.7
Arkansas (16)	3.3	Maryland (44)	1.1	Oregon (20)	2.6
California (26)	2.2	Massachusetts (50)	0.5	Pennsylvania (42)	1.3
Colorado (13)	3.4	Michigan (29)	2.1	Rhode Island (45)	1.0
Connecticut (48)	0.8	Minnesota (35)	1.8	South Carolina (41)	1.4
Delaware (13)	3.4	Mississippi (26)	2.2	South Dakota (1)	5.4
D.C. (51)	0.2	Missouri (12)	3.5	Tennessee (31)	2.0
Florida (45)	1.0	Montana (2)	5.3	Texas (20)	2.6
Georgia (29)	2.1	Nebraska (11)	3.6	Utah (22)	2.5
Hawaii (24)	2.3	Nevada (31)	2.0	Vermont (6)	4.0
Idaho (5)	4.2	New Hampshire (24)	2.3	Virginia (39)	1.5
Illinois (35)	1.8	New Jersey (48)	0.8	Washington (31)	2.0
Indiana (37)	1.7	New Mexico (18)	2.7	West Virginia (22)	2.5
Iowa (9)	3.7	New York (47)	0.9	Wisconsin (7)	3.8
Kansas (17)	3.1	North Carolina (26)	2.2	Wyoming (3)	4.6

SOURCE: Compiled from state tables in *State Higher Education Profiles*, National Center for Education Statistics, 1988.

Table 3.12

Bachelor's Degrees Conferred in Engineering
(proportion of degrees conferred, 1987)

Alabama (15)	10.6%	Kentucky (41)	7.0%	North Dakota (10)	11.5%
Alaska (5)	13.4	Louisiana (9)	11.6	Ohio (17)	10.0
Arizona (6)	12.7	Maine (28)	8.4	Oklahoma (22)	9.3
Arkansas (51)	4.7	Maryland (43)	6.7	Oregon (32)	8.0
California (18)	9.6	Massachusetts (12)	11.3	Pennsylvania (20)	9.4
Colorado (13)	10.9	Michigan (7)	12.6	Rhode Island (45)	6.3
Connecticut (32)	8.0	Minnesota (47)	5.2	South Carolina (38)	7.2
Delaware (39)	7.1	Mississippi (27)	8.8	South Dakota (4)	14.0
D.C. (42)	6.9	Missouri (23)	9.1	Tennessee (11)	11.4
Florida (16)	10.5	Montana (3)	14.2	Texas (26)	8.9
Georgia (23)	9.1	Nebraska (48)	4.9	Utah (14)	10.8
Hawaii (46)	5.7	Nevada (32)	8.0	Vermont (50)	4.8
Idaho (31)	8.1	New Hampshire (48)	4.9	Virginia (37)	7.5
Illinois (29)	8.3	New Jersey (23)	9.1	Washington (32)	8.0
Indiana (8)	12.3	New Mexico (2)	15.0	West Virginia (20)	9.4
Iowa (39)	7.1	New York (36)	7.7	Wisconsin (18)	9.6
Kansas (30)	8.2	North Carolina (44)	6.6	Wyoming (1)	15.1

SOURCE: Compiled from state tables in *State Higher Education Profiles*, National Center for Education Statistics, 1988.

Table 3.13

Bachelor's Degrees Conferred in the Social Sciences
(proportion of degrees conferred, 1987)

Alabama (44)	5.5%	Kentucky (36)	6.8%	North Dakota (49)	4.2%
Alaska (42)	5.6	Louisiana (41)	5.9	Ohio (32)	7.2
Arizona (31)	7.3	Maine (10)	13.0	Oklahoma (42)	5.6
Arkansas (49)	4.2	Maryland (13)	11.7	Oregon (17)	10.5
California (11)	12.7	Massachusetts (3)	15.6	Pennsylvania (24)	9.1
Colorado (16)	10.6	Michigan (29)	7.5	Rhode Island (21)	9.7
Connecticut (4)	14.4	Minnesota (20)	10.1	South Carolina (19)	10.2
Delaware (4)	14.4	Mississippi (48)	4.4	South Dakota (18)	10.4
D.C. (1)	22.3	Missouri (45)	5.4	Tennessee (30)	7.4
Florida (28)	7.6	Montana (33)	7.0	Texas (33)	7.0
Georgia (26)	8.5	Nebraska (46)	5.0	Utah (14)	11.0
Hawaii (15)	10.8	Nevada (40)	6.0	Vermont (2)	17.6
Idaho (35)	6.9	New Hampshire (8)	13.5	Virginia (6)	14.3
Illinois (25)	9.0	New Jersey (7)	13.7	Washington (22)	9.5
Indiana (27)	7.9	New Mexico (38)	6.5	West Virginia (47)	4.6
Iowa (36)	6.8	New York (12)	12.0	Wisconsin (22)	9.5
Kansas (39)	6.2	North Carolina (9)	13.3	Wyoming (49)	4.2

SOURCE: Compiled from state tables in *State Higher Education Profiles*, National Center for Education Statistics, 1988.

Table 3.14

Average Faculty Salary
(all ranks, four-year institutions, 1989–90)

Alabama (42)	$33,308	Kentucky (44)	$32,714	North Dakota (47)	$30,907
Alaska (5)	44,789	Louisiana (43)	33,275	Ohio (16)	40,141
Arizona (13)	40,903	Maine (29)	36,794	Oklahoma (38)	34,508
Arkansas (46)	31,588	Maryland (9)	41,806	Oregon (40)	34,342
California (2)	46,476	Massachusetts (3)	46,113	Pennsylvania (11)	41,177
Colorado (22)	38,450	Michigan (10)	41,270	Rhode Island (8)	43,972
Connecticut (1)	47,230	Minnesota (19)	39,376	South Carolina (41)	34,017
Delaware (14)	40,682	Mississippi (48)	30,595	South Dakota (51)	29,437
D.C. (6)	44,708	Missouri (34)	35,621	Tennessee (32)	36,126
Florida (25)	38,027	Montana (49)	29,780	Texas (26)	37,615
Georgia (31)	36,261	Nebraska (35)	34,745	Utah (23)	38,319
Hawaii (17)	39,917	Nevada (18)	39,414	Vermont (33)	36,018
Idaho (45)	32,118	New Hampshire (20)	38,783	Virginia (12)	40,984
Illinois (15)	40,546	New Jersey (4)	45,136	Washington (30)	36,675
Indiana (27)	37,442	New Mexico (36)	34,661	West Virginia (50)	29,758
Iowa (24)	38,028	New York (7)	44,557	Wisconsin (21)	38,463
Kansas (37)	34,629	North Carolina (28)	37,207	Wyoming (39)	34,438

SOURCE: *Salaries of Full-Time Instructional Faculty on 9- and 10-Month Contracts in Institutions of Higher Education, 1979–80 through 1989–90* (Washington, D.C.: National Center for Education Statistics, 1991), p. 12.

Table 3.15

Average Female Faculty Salary as a Percentage of Male Salary
(all ranks, 1989–90)

Alabama (22)	79%	Kentucky (10)	81%	North Dakota (10)	81%
Alaska (1)	92	Louisiana (41)	77	Ohio (37)	78
Arizona (22)	79	Maine (22)	79	Oklahoma (4)	83
Arkansas (22)	79	Maryland (22)	79	Oregon (6)	82
California (10)	81	Massachusetts (22)	79	Pennsylvania (37)	78
Colorado (10)	81	Michigan (41)	77	Rhode Island (37)	78
Connecticut (22)	79	Minnesota (10)	81	South Carolina (37)	78
Delaware (49)	75	Mississippi (22)	79	South Dakota (10)	81
D.C. (19)	80	Missouri (22)	79	Tennessee (44)	76
Florida (22)	79	Montana (2)	85	Texas (44)	76
Georgia (22)	79	Nebraska (22)	79	Utah (4)	83
Hawaii (19)	80	Nevada (10)	81	Vermont (22)	79
Idaho (2)	85	New Hampshire (22)	79	Virginia (41)	77
Illinois (44)	76	New Jersey (6)	82	Washington (10)	81
Indiana (49)	75	New Mexico (6)	82	West Virginia (6)	82
Iowa (44)	76	New York (10)	81	Wisconsin (12)	79
Kansas (44)	76	North Carolina (19)	80	Wyoming (51)	74

SOURCE: Calculated from tables 18 and 19, *Salaries of Full-Time Instructional Faculty on 9- and 10-Month Contracts in Institutions of Higher Education, 1979–80 through 1989–90* (Washington, D.C.: National Center for Education Statistics, 1991), pp. 23, 24.

Table 3.16

Student-Faculty Ratio
(FTE students and FTE instructional staff, 1989)

Alabama (46)	16.7	Kentucky (41)	16.3	North Dakota (23)	13.2
Alaska (31)	14.7	Louisiana (29)	14.2	Ohio (24)	13.4
Arizona (49)	19.7	Maine (51)	24.2	Oklahoma (31)	14.7
Arkansas (29)	14.2	Maryland (22)	13.0	Oregon (5)	10.5
California (43)	16.4	Massachusetts (37)	15.3	Pennsylvania (48)	19.6
Colorado (2)	9.4	Michigan (36)	15.0	Rhode Island (7)	11.0
Connecticut (43)	16.4	Minnesota (15)	12.4	South Carolina (12)	12.1
Delaware (12)	12.1	Mississippi (14)	12.3	South Dakota (27)	14.0
D.C. (16)	12.5	Missouri (26)	13.8	Tennessee (20)	12.8
Florida (31)	14.7	Montana (34)	14.8	Texas (41)	16.3
Georgia (9)	11.9	Nebraska (39)	15.9	Utah (6)	10.6
Hawaii (16)	12.5	Nevada (50)	23.8	Vermont (8)	11.4
Idaho (9)	11.9	New Hampshire (24)	13.4	Virginia (21)	12.9
Illinois (37)	15.3	New Jersey (39)	15.9	Washington (11)	12.0
Indiana (16)	12.5	New Mexico (27)	14.0	West Virginia (34)	14.8
Iowa (3)	9.7	New York (43)	16.4	Wisconsin (16)	12.5
Kansas (47)	17.8	North Carolina (3)	9.7	Wyoming (1)	6.7

SOURCE: Calculated from table 190, *Digest of Education Statistics, 1991*, and table C-2, *Rankings of the States, 1991* (West Haven, Conn. National Education Association, 1991).

Table 4.1

Percentage of Minorities in Higher Education, 1990

Alabama (15)	20.9%	Kentucky (39)	7.4%	North Dakota (41)	6.2%
Alaska (19)	17.1	Louisiana (7)	27.7	Ohio (32)	10.7
Arizona (17)	19.7	Maine (51)	2.3	Oklahoma (21)	15.6
Arkansas (23)	15.3	Maryland (9)	23.5	Oregon (37)	7.9
California (4)	32.4	Massachusetts (29)	11.5	Pennsylvania (31)	11.0
Colorado (26)	13.8	Michigan (25)	14.1	Rhode Island (36)	8.0
Connecticut (28)	12.0	Minnesota (45)	5.1	South Carolina (14)	21.3
Delaware (24)	14.4	Mississippi (6)	28.7	South Dakota (40)	7.2
D.C. (2)	38.0	Missouri (30)	11.1	Tennessee (21)	15.6
Florida (10)	23.1	Montana (35)	8.2	Texas (5)	28.8
Georgia (11)	22.5	Nebraska (43)	5.5	Utah (44)	5.3
Hawaii (1)	63.2	Nevada (20)	16.1	Vermont (49)	4.1
Idaho (48)	4.8	New Hampshire (50)	3.6	Virginia (18)	18.9
Illinois (8)	23.7	New Jersey (13)	21.6	Washington (27)	12.4
Indiana (34)	8.6	New Mexico (3)	36.8	West Virginia (45)	5.1
Iowa (47)	5.0	New York (10)	23.1	Wisconsin (38)	7.5
Kansas (33)	9.2	North Carolina (16)	20.8	Wyoming (42)	5.8

SOURCE: Calculated from *Trends in Racial/Ethnic Enrollment in Higher Education: Fall 1980 through Fall 1990*, January 1992, National Center for Education Statistics, table 6.

Table 4.2

African-Americans in Higher Education
(percentage of total enrollment, 1990)

Alabama (5)	19.5%	Kentucky (24)	5.9%	North Dakota (47)	0.6%
Alaska (31)	3.6	Louisiana (3)	24.0	Ohio (19)	8.1
Arizona (35)	2.9	Maine (49)	0.5	Oklahoma (22)	6.8
Arkansas (11)	13.5	Maryland (8)	16.8	Oregon (42)	1.3
California (23)	6.5	Massachusetts (28)	4.4	Pennsylvania (21)	7.3
Colorado (34)	3.0	Michigan (16)	10.0	Rhode Island (33)	3.3
Connecticut (24)	5.9	Minnesota (41)	1.6	South Carolina (4)	19.6
Delaware (13)	11.2	Mississippi (2)	27.4	South Dakota (46)	0.7
D.C. (1)	30.7	Missouri (20)	8.0	Tennessee (10)	13.8
Florida (17)	9.9	Montana (51)	0.3	Texas (18)	8.9
Georgia (5)	19.5	Nebraska (39)	2.4	Utah (49)	0.5
Hawaii (37)	2.7	Nevada (27)	4.7	Vermont (44)	1.0
Idaho (47)	0.6	New Hampshire (43)	1.1	Virginia (9)	14.0
Illinois (12)	12.2	New Jersey (15)	10.2	Washington (36)	2.8
Indiana (26)	5.4	New Mexico (38)	2.5	West Virginia (30)	3.7
Iowa (39)	2.4	New York (14)	10.8	Wisconsin (31)	3.6
Kansas (29)	4.2	North Carolina (7)	17.6	Wyoming (45)	0.9

SOURCE: Calculated from *Trends in Racial/Ethnic Enrollment in Higher Education: Fall 1980 through Fall 1990*, National Center for Education Statistics, table 6.

Table 4.3
Predominantly Black Institutions, 1990

Historically Black Colleges and Universities

ALABAMA
   Alabama A&M University
   Alabama State University
   S.D. Bishop State Community College
   Carver State Technical College
   Concordia College
   Lawson State Community College
   Miles College
   Oakwood College
   Selma University
   Stillman College
   Talladega College
   Trenholm State Technical College
   Tuskegee University
ARKANSAS
   Arkansas Baptist College
   Philander Smith College
   Shorter College
   University of Arkansas, Pine Bluff
DELAWARE
   Delaware State College
District of Columbia
   Howard University
   University of the District of Columbia
FLORIDA
   Bethune-Cookman College
   Edward Waters College
   Florida A&M University
   Florida Memorial College
GEORGIA
   Albany State College
   Clark Atlanta University
   Fort Valley State College
   Morehouse College
   Morehouse School of Medicine
   Morris Brown College
   Paine College
   Savannah State College
   Spelman College
KENTUCKY
   Kentucky State University
   Simmons University Bible College
LOUISIANA
   Dillard University
   Grambling State University
   Southern University System
   Southern University at Baton Rouge
   Southern University at New Orleans

Southern University at Shreveport
   Xavier University
MARYLAND
   Bowie State University
   Coppin State College
   Morgan State University
   University of Maryland Eastern Shore
MICHIGAN
   Lewis College of Business
MISSISSIPPI
   Alcorn State University
   Coahoma Community College
   Jackson State University
   Mary Holmes College
   Mississippi Valley State University
   Natchez Junior College
   Prentiss Institute Junior College
   Rust College
   Tougaloo College
   Utica Campus-Hinds Junior College
MISSOURI
   Harris-Stowe State College
   Lincoln University
NORTH CAROLINA
   Barber-Scotia College
   Bennett College
   Elizabeth City State University
   Fayetteville State University
   Johnson C. Smith University
   Livingston College
   North Carolina A&T State University
   North Carolina Central University
   Saint Augustine's College
   Shaw University
   Winston-Salem State University
OHIO
   Central State University
   Wilberforce University
OKLAHOMA
   Langston University
PENNSYLVANIA
   Cheyney University
   Lincoln University
SOUTH CAROLINA
   Allen University
   Benedict College
   Claflin College
   Clinton Junior College

Table 4.3 (cont.)

Denmark Technical College	*VIRGINIA*
Morris College	Hampton University
South Carolina State College	Norfolk State University
Voorhees College	Saint Paul's College
TENNESSEE	The Virginia Seminary and College
Fisk University	Virginia State University
Knoxville College	Virginia Union University
Lane College	*WEST VIRGINIA*
LeMoyne–Owen College	West Virginia State College
Meharry Medical College	*OTHER EQUAL OPPORTUNITY EDUCATIONAL*
Morristown College (closed)	*COLLEGES AND UNIVERSITIES*
Tennessee State University	Atlanta Metropolitan College
TEXAS	Chicago State University
Bishop College (closed)	Compton Community College
Huston–Tillotson College	Cuyahoga Community College
Jarvis Christian College	Charles R. Drew University of Medicine and Science
Paul Quinn College	Highland Park Community College
Prairie View A&M University	Kennedy-King College
Southwestern Christian College	Medgar Evers College
Texas College	Roxbury Community College
Texas Southern University	Sojourner-Douglass College
Wiley College	Wayne County Community College

SOURCE: National Association for Equal Opportunity in Higher Education, 1990.

Table 4.4

Hispanics in Higher Education
(percentage of total enrollment, 1990)

Alabama (44)	0.5%	Kentucky (47)	0.4%	North Dakota (44)	0.5%
Alaska (17)	2.1	Louisiana (22)	1.8	Ohio (36)	1.0
Arizona (4)	11.2	Maine (49)	0.3	Oklahoma (27)	1.5
Arkansas (44)	0.5	Maryland (19)	1.9	Oregon (22)	1.8
California (3)	12.6	Massachusetts (12)	3.0	Pennsylvania (31)	1.3
Colorado (6)	7.5	Michigan (25)	1.6	Rhode Island (17)	2.1
Connecticut (11)	3.3	Minnesota (38)	0.8	South Carolina (42)	0.6
Delaware (31)	1.3	Mississippi (49)	0.3	South Dakota (49)	0.3
D.C. (12)	3.0	Missouri (33)	1.2	Tennessee (42)	0.6
Florida (5)	10.9	Montana (38)	0.8	Texas (2)	16.5
Georgia (35)	1.1	Nebraska (29)	1.4	Utah (22)	1.8
Hawaii (19)	1.9	Nevada (10)	5.5	Vermont (33)	1.2
Idaho (19)	1.9	New Hampshire (38)	0.8	Virginia (29)	1.4
Illinois (8)	6.7	New Jersey (8)	6.7	Washington (15)	2.3
Indiana (27)	1.5	New Mexico (1)	27.6	West Virginia (25)	1.6
Iowa (37)	0.9	New York (7)	7.2	Wisconsin (47)	0.4
Kansas (16)	2.2	North Carolina (41)	0.7	Wyoming (14)	2.9

SOURCE: Calculated from *Trends in Racial/Ethnic Enrollment in Higher Education: Fall 1980 through Fall 1990*, January 1992, National Center for Education Statistics, table 6.

Table 4.5
Hispanic-Serving Institutions
(institutions with more than 25% Hispanic enrollment, 1990)

ARIZONA
  Arizona Western College
  South Mountain Community College
CALIFORNIA
  California State University, Los Angeles
  Cerritos College
  Compton Community College
  Don Bosco Technical Institute
  East Los Angeles College
  Gavilan College
  Hartnell College
  Imperial Valley College
  Kings River Community College
  Los Angeles City College
  Los Angeles Mission College
  Los Angeles Trade-Technical College
  Mount Saint Mary's College
  Mt. San Antonio College
  Oxnard College
  Palo Verde College
  Rio Hondo College
  Saint John's Seminary College
  Southwestern College
  West Coast Christian College
  West Hills Community College
COLORADO
  Pueblo Community College
  Trinidad State Junior College
FLORIDA
  Harry University
  Florida International University
  Miami-Dade Community College
  Saint John Vianney College Seminary
  St. Thomas University
  Saint Vincent de Paul Regional Seminary
ILLINOIS
  MacCormac Junior College
  St. Augustine College
  Harry S. Truman College
NEW JERSEY
  Hudson County Community College
  Passaic County Community College
NEW MEXICO
  Albuquerque Technical-Vocational Institute

College of Santa Fe
Dona Ana Branch Community College
Eastern New Mexico University–Roswell
New Mexico Highlands University
New Mexico State University
New Mexico State University, Grants
Northern New Mexico Community College
Santa Fe Community College
University of New Mexico, Valencia
Western New Mexico University

NEW YORK
  Boricua College
  Borough of Manhattan Community College
  Bronx Community College
  College of Aeronautics
  Hostos Community College
  John Jay College of Criminal Justice
  LaGuardia Community College
  Herbert H. Lehman College
  Mercy College

TEXAS
  Bee County College
  Corpus Christi State University
  Del Mar College
  El Paso County Community College
  Incarnate Word College
  Laredo Junior College
  Laredo State University
  Our Lady of the Lake University
  Palo Alto College
  St. Mary's University
  St. Philip's College
  San Antonio College
  Southwest Texas Junior College
  Sul Ross State University
  Texas A&I University
  Texas Southmost College
  Texas State Technical Institute-Harlingen
  University of Texas at El Paso
  University of Texas at San Antonio
  University of Texas-Pan American
  University of Texas-Pan American at Brownsville

SOURCE: Hispanic Association of Colleges and Universities, Annual Report, 1990.

Table 4.6

Asians in Higher Education
(percentage of total enrollment, 1990)

Alabama (46)	0.7%	Kentucky (42)	0.8%	North Dakota (42)	0.8%
Alaska (15)	2.5	Louisiana (32)	1.4	Ohio (36)	1.3
Arizona (17)	2.3	Maine (46)	0.7	Oklahoma (24)	1.7
Arkansas (42)	0.8	Maryland (5)	4.4	Oregon (11)	3.8
California (2)	12.2	Massachusetts (10)	3.9	Pennsylvania (19)	2.2
Colorado (17)	2.3	Michigan (21)	1.9	Rhode Island (16)	2.4
Connecticut (14)	2.6	Minnesota (21)	1.9	South Carolina (39)	0.9
Delaware (24)	1.7	Mississippi (48)	0.6	South Dakota (48)	0.6
D.C. (9)	4.0	Missouri (29)	1.6	Tennessee (37)	1.0
Florida (20)	2.0	Montana (51)	0.3	Texas (13)	3.1
Georgia (24)	1.7	Nebraska (39)	1.0	Utah (23)	1.8
Hawaii (1)	58.3	Nevada (8)	4.1	Vermont (29)	1.6
Idaho (32)	1.4	New Hampshire (36)	1.3	Virginia (12)	3.2
Illinois (5)	4.4	New Jersey (5)	4.4	Washington (3)	5.9
Indiana (32)	1.4	New Mexico (36)	1.3	West Virginia (42)	0.8
Iowa (32)	1.4	New York (4)	4.7	Wisconsin (24)	1.7
Kansas (24)	1.7	North Carolina (27)	1.6	Wyoming (50)	0.6

SOURCE: Calculated from *Trends in Racial/Ethnic Enrollment in Higher Education: Fall 1980 through Fall 1990*, National Center for Education Statistics, table 6.

Table 4.7

Native Americans in Higher Education
(percentage of total enrollment, 1990)

Alabama (43)	0.2%	Kentucky (29)	0.3%	North Dakota (6)	4.3%
Alaska (1)	8.9	Louisiana (23)	0.5	Ohio (29)	0.3
Arizona (7)	3.3	Maine (19)	0.7	Oklahoma (4)	5.5
Arkansas (23)	0.5	Maryland (29)	0.3	Oregon (14)	1.0
California (11)	1.2	Massachusetts (29)	0.3	Pennsylvania (43)	0.2
Colorado (14)	1.0	Michigan (21)	0.6	Rhode Island (29)	0.3
Connecticut (29)	0.3	Minnesota (18)	0.8	South Carolina (43)	0.2
Delaware (43)	0.2	Mississippi (29)	0.3	South Dakota (3)	5.6
D.C. (29)	0.3	Missouri (25)	0.4	Tennessee (43)	0.2
Florida (29)	0.3	Montana (2)	6.8	Texas (29)	0.3
Georgia (43)	0.2	Nebraska (21)	0.6	Utah (13)	1.1
Hawaii (29)	0.3	Nevada (8)		Vermont (25)	0.4
Idaho (16)	0.9	New Hampshire (25)	0.4	Virginia (43)	0.2
Illinois (29)	0.3	New Jersey (43)	0.2	Washington (9)	1.5
Indiana (29)	0.3	New Mexico (5)	5.4	West Virginia (43)	0.2
Iowa (29)	0.3	New York (25)	0.4	Wisconsin (19)	0.7
Kansas (11)	1.2	North Carolina (16)	0.9	Wyoming (10)	1.4

SOURCE: Calculated from *Trends in Racial/Ethnic Enrollment in Higher Education: Fall 1980 through Fall 1990*, National Center for Education Statistics, table 6.

Table 4.8

Native American Colleges, 1992

Bay Mills Community College Brimley, Michigan	*Navajo Community College* Tsaile, Arizona
Blackfeet Community College Browning, Montana	*Nebraska Indian Community College* Winnebago, Nebraska
Cheyenne River Community College Eagle Butte, South Dakota	*Northwest Indian College* Bellingham, Washington
Crownpoint Institute of Technology Crownpoint, New Mexico	*Oglala Lakota College* Kyle, South Dakota
DQ University Davis, California	*Lac Courte Orielles Ojibwa Community College* Hayward, Wisconsin
Dull Knife Memorial College Lame Deer, Montana	*Salish Kootenai College* Pablo, Montana
Fond du Lac Community College Cloquet, Minnesota	*Sinte Gleska University* Rosebud, South Dakota
Fort Belknap Community College Harlem, Montana	*Southwest Indian Polytechnic Institute* Albuquerque, New Mexico
Fort Berthold Community College New Town, North Dakota	*Standing Rock College* Fort Yates, North Dakota
Fort Peck Community College Poplar, Montana	*Stone Child Community College* Box Elder, Montana
Haskell Indian Junior College Lawrence, Kansas	*Turtle Mountain Community College* Belcourt, North Dakota
Little Big Horn College Crow Agency, Montana	*United Tribes Technical School* Bismarck, North Dakota
Little Hoop Community College Fort Totten, North Dakota	

SOURCE: *Tribal College*, the Journal of American Indian Higher Education, 1992.

Table 5.1
ABA-Approved Law Schools, 1991

ALABAMA
University of Alabama School of Law
Cumberland School of Law of Samford
    University
ARIZONA
University of Arizona College of Law
Arizona State University College of Law
ARKANSAS
University of Arkansas, Fayetteville, Leflar Law
    Center
University of Arkansas at Little Rock School of
    Law
CALIFORNIA
University of California at Berkeley School of
    Law
University of California at Davis School of Law
University of California at Hastings College of
    Law
University of California at Los Angeles School
    of Law
California Western School of Law
Golden Gate University School of Law
Loyola Law School
McGeorge School of Law, University of the
    Pacific
Pepperdine University School of Law
University of San Diego School of Law
University of San Francisco School of Law
Santa Clara University School of Law
University of Southern California Law Center
Southwestern University School of Law
Stanford Law School
Whittier College School of Law
COLORADO
University of Colorado School of Law
University of Denver College of Law
CONNECTICUT
University of Bridgeport School of Law
University of Connecticut School of Law
Yale Law School
DELAWARE
Widener University School of Law
District of Columbia
American University, Washington College of
    Law
Catholic University of America School of Law
Georgetown University Law Center
George Washington University National Law
    Center
Howard University School of Law

FLORIDA
University of Florida College of Law
Florida State University College of Law
University of Miami School of Law
Nova University Shepard Broad Law Center
Stetson University College of Law
GEORGIA
Emory University School of Law
University of Georgia School of Law
Mercer University Law School
HAWAII
University of Hawaii William S. Richardson
    School of Law
IDAHO
University of Idaho College of Law
ILLINOIS
University of Chicago Law School
DePaul University College of Law
University of Illinois College of Law
Illinois Institute of Technology, Chicago–Kent
    College
Loyola University School of Law, Chicago
John Marshall Law School
Northern Illinois University College of Law
Northwestern University School of Law
Southern Illinois University School of Law
INDIANA
Indiana University at Bloomington School of
    Law
Indiana University School of Law,
    Indianapolis
Notre Dame Law School
Valparaiso University School of Law
IOWA
Drake University Law School
University of Iowa College of Law
KANSAS
University of Kansas School of Law
Washburn University School of Law
KENTUCKY
University of Kentucky College of Law
University of Louisville School of Law
Northern Kentucky University, Salmon P.
    Chase College of Law
LOUISIANA
Louisiana State University Law Center
Loyola University School of Law, New Orleans
Tulane University School of Law
MAINE
University of Maine School of Law

MARYLAND
    University of Baltimore School of Law
    University of Maryland School of Law
MASSACHUSETTS
    Boston College Law School
    Boston University School of Law
    Harvard University Law School
    Northeastern University School of Law
    Suffolk University Law School
    Western New England College School of Law
MICHIGAN
    Detroit College of Law
    University of Michigan Law School
    Wayne State University Law School
MINNESOTA
    Hamline University School of Law
    University of Minnesota Law School
    William Mitchell College of Law
MISSISSIPPI
    Mississippi College School of Law
    University of Mississippi School of Law
MISSOURI
    University of Missouri–Columbia, School of Law
    University of Missouri–Kansas City, School of Law
    Saint Louis University School of Law
    Washington University School of Law
MONTANA
    University of Montana School of Law
NEBRASKA
    Creighton University School of Law
    University of Nebraska College of Law
NEW JERSEY
    Rutgers University School of Law, Camden
    Rutgers University, S.I. Newhouse Center for Law and Justice
    Seton Hall University School of Law
NEW MEXICO
    University of New Mexico School of Law
NEW YORK
    Albany Law School, Union University
    Brooklyn Law School
    Columbia University School of Law
    Cornell Law School
    Fordham University School of Law
    Hofstra University School of Law
    State University of New York at Buffalo School of Law
    New York Law School

New York University School of Law
Pace University School of Law
St. John's University School of Law
Syracuse University College of Law
Yeshiva University, Benjamin N. Cardozo School of Law
NORTH CAROLINA
    Duke University School of Law (Trinity College)
    University of North Carolina School of Law
    Wake Forest University School of Law
NORTH DAKOTA
    University of North Dakota School of Law
OHIO
    University of Akron
    Capital University Law School
    Case Western Reserve University Law School
    University of Cincinnati College of Law
    Cleveland State University
    University of Dayton School of Law
    Ohio Northern University, Pettit College of Law
    Ohio State University College of Law
    University of Toledo College of Law
OKLAHOMA
    University of Oklahoma Law Center
    University of Tulsa College of Law
OREGON
    Lewis and Clark Northwestern School of Law
    University of Oregon School of Law
    Willamette University College of Law
PENNSYLVANIA
    Dickinson School of Law
    Duquesne University School of Law
    University of Pennsylvania Law School
    University of Pittsburgh School of Law
    Temple University School of Law
    Villanova University School of Law
SOUTH CAROLINA
    University of South Carolina School of Law
SOUTH DAKOTA
    University of South Dakota School of Law
TENNESSEE
    University of Tennessee College of Law
    Vanderbilt University School of Law
TEXAS
    Baylor University School of Law
    University of Houston Law Center
    St. Mary's University of San Antonio School of Law

Table 5.1 (cont.)

TEXAS *(cont.)*
    Southern Methodist University School of Law
    University of Texas School of Law
    Texas Tech University School of Law
UTAH
    Brigham Young University, J. Reuben Clark
        Law School
    University of Utah College of Law
VERMONT
    Vermont Law School
VIRGINIA
    George Mason University School of Law
    University of Richmond, T. C. Williams
        School of Law

University of Virginia School of Law
Washington and Lee University School of Law
College of William and Mary, Marshall-Wythe
    School of Law
WASHINGTON
    Gonzaga University School of Law
    University of Puget Sound School of Law
    University of Washington School of Law
WEST VIRGINIA
    West Virginia University College of Law
WISCONSIN
    University of Wisconsin Law School
WYOMING
    University of Wyoming College of Law

SOURCE: American Bar Association, 1991.

Table 5.2
Accredited Medical Schools, 1991

ALABAMA
    University of Alabama
    University of South Alabama
ARIZONA
    University of Arizona
ARKANSAS
    University of Arkansas
CALIFORNIA
    University of California, Davis
    University of California, Irvine
    University of California, Los Angeles
    Drew/UCLA
    University of California, San Diego
    University of California, San Francisco
    Loma Linda University
    University of Southern California
    Stanford University
COLORADO
    University of Colorado
CONNECTICUT
    University of Connecticut
    Yale University
District of Columbia
    George Washington University
    Georgetown University
    Howard University
FLORIDA
    University of Florida

    University of Miami
    University of South Florida
GEORGIA
    Emory University
    Medical College of Georgia
    Mercer University
    Morehouse School of Medicine
HAWAII
    University of Hawaii
ILLINOIS
    University of Chicago
    UHS/Chicago Medical School
    University of Illinois
    Loyola University of Chicago
    Northwestern University
    Rush Medical College
    Southern Illinois University
INDIANA
    Indiana University
IOWA
    University of Iowa
KANSAS
    University of Kansas
KENTUCKY
    University of Kentucky
    University of Louisville
LOUISIANA
    Louisiana State University–New Orleans

230

Louisiana State University–Shreveport
Tulane University
MARYLAND
Johns Hopkins University
University of Maryland
Uniformed Services University of the Health
Sciences
MASSACHUSETTS
Boston University
Harvard University
University of Massachusetts
Tufts University
MICHIGAN
Michigan State University
University of Michigan
Wayne State University
MINNESOTA
Mayo Medical School
University of Minnesota–Duluth
University of Minnesota–Minneapolis
MISSISSIPPI
University of Mississippi
MISSOURI
University of Missouri–Columbia
University of Missouri–Kansas City
Saint Louis University
Washington University
NEBRASKA
Creighton University
University of Nebraska
NEVADA
University of Nevada
NEW HAMPSHIRE
Dartmouth Medical School
NEW JERSEY
UMDNJ–New Jersey Medical School
UMDNJ–R.W. Johnson Medical School
NEW MEXICO
University of New Mexico
NEW YORK
Albany Medical College
Albert Einstein College of Medicine
Columbia University
Cornell University
Mount Sinai School of Medicine
New York Medical College
New York University
University of Rochester
SUNY–Brooklyn
SUNY–Buffalo

SUNY–Stony Brook
SUNY–Syracuse
NORTH CAROLINA
Bowman Gray School of
Medicine of Wake Forest University
Duke University
East Carolina University
University of North Carolina
NORTH DAKOTA
University of North Dakota
OHIO
Case Western Reserve University
University of Cincinnati
Medical College of Ohio
Northeastern Ohio Universities
Ohio State University
Wright State University
OKLAHOMA
University of Oklahoma
OREGON
Oregon Health Sciences University
PENNSYLVANIA
Hahnemann University
Jefferson Medical College of
Thomas Jefferson University
Medical College of Pennsylvania
Pennsylvania State University
University of Pennsylvania
University of Pittsburgh
Temple University
RHODE ISLAND
Brown University
SOUTH CAROLINA
Medical University of South Carolina
University of South Carolina
SOUTH DAKOTA
University of South Dakota
TENNESSEE
East Tennessee State University
Meharry Medical College
University of Tennessee
Vanderbilt University
TEXAS
Baylor College of Medicine
Texas A&M University
Texas Tech University
University of Texas–Dallas
University of Texas–Galveston
University of Texas–Houston
University of Texas–San Antonio

Table 5.2 (cont.)

UTAH	**WASHINGTON**
University of Utah	University of Washington
VERMONT	**WEST VIRGINIA**
University of Vermont	Marshall University
VIRGINIA	West Virginia University
Eastern Virginia Medical School	**WISCONSIN**
Medical College of Virginia at Virginia Commonwealth University	Medical College of Wisconsin
	University of Wisconsin Medical School
University of Virginia	

SOURCE: Association of American Medical Colleges, 1991.

Table 5.3
Accredited Colleges of Veterinary Medicine, 1991

ALABAMA	**MISSISSIPPI**
Auburn University	Mississippi State University
Tuskegee Institute	**MISSOURI**
CALIFORNIA	University of Missouri
University of California at Davis	**NEW YORK**
COLORADO	Cornell University
Colorado State University	**NORTH CAROLINA**
FLORIDA	North Carolina State University
University of Florida	**OHIO**
GEORGIA	Ohio State University
University of Georgia	**OKLAHOMA**
ILLINOIS	Oklahoma State University
University of Illinois	**OREGON**
INDIANA	Oregon State University
Purdue University	**PENNSYLVANIA**
IOWA	University of Pennsylvania
Iowa State University	**TENNESSEE**
KANSAS	University of Tennessee
Kansas State University	**TEXAS**
LOUISIANA	Texas A&M University
Louisiana State University	**VIRGINIA**
MASSACHUSETTS	Virginia Polytechnic Institute and State University
Tufts University	**WASHINGTON**
MICHIGAN	Washington State University
Michigan State University	**WISCONSIN**
MINNESOTA	University of Wisconsin
University of Minnesota	

SOURCE: American Veterinary Medical Association, 1991.

Table 5.4

Accredited Dental Schools, 1991

ALABAMA	*MISSOURI*
University of Alabama	University of Missouri–Kansas City
CALIFORNIA	Washington University, St. Louis
Loma Linda University	*NEBRASKA*
University of the Pacific	Creighton University
University of California, Los Angeles	University of Nebraska, Omaha
University of California, San Francisco	*NEW JERSEY*
University of Southern California	Fairleigh Dickinson University
COLORADO	University of Medicine and Dentistry of New Jersey
University of Colorado	*NEW YORK*
CONNECTICUT	Columbia University
University of Connecticut	New York University
District of Columbia	SUNY–Buffalo
Howard University	SUNY–Stony Brook
FLORIDA	*NORTH CAROLINA*
University of Florida	University of North Carolina
GEORGIA	*OHIO*
Medical College of Georgia	Case Western Reserve University
HAWAII	Ohio State University
University of Hawaii	*OKLAHOMA*
ILLINOIS	University of Oklahoma
Loyola University	*OREGON*
Northwestern University	Oregon Health Sciences University
Southern Illinois University	*PENNSYLVANIA*
University of Illinois	Temple University
INDIANA	University of Pennsylvania
Indiana University	University of Pittsburgh
IOWA	*SOUTH CAROLINA*
University of Iowa	Medical University of South Carolina
KENTUCKY	*TENNESSEE*
University of Kentucky	Meharry Medical College
University of Louisville	University of Tennessee
LOUISIANA	*TEXAS*
Louisiana State University	Baylor College of Dentistry
MARYLAND	University of Texas–Houston
University of Maryland	University of Texas–San Antonio
MASSACHUSETTS	*VIRGINIA*
Boston University	Virginia Commonwealth University
Harvard University	*WASHINGTON*
Tufts University	University of Washington, Seattle
MICHIGAN	*WEST VIRGINIA*
University of Detroit	West Virginia University
University of Michigan	*WISCONSIN*
MINNESOTA	Marquette University
University of Minnesota	
MISSISSIPPI	
University of Mississippi	

SOURCE: American Association of Dental Schools, 1991.

Table 5.5

Institutions Granting the Largest Number of Doctoral Degrees, 1979–88

Top Twenty-Five Institutions in Doctoral Degrees Granted	Total 1978–79 to 1987–88
1. University of California, Berkeley	7,139
2. University of Wisconsin, Madison	6,521
3. University of Michigan, Ann Arbor	6,066
4. University of Illinois, Urbana	5,963
5. Columbia University	5,939
6. Ohio State University	5,508
7. Stanford University	5,046
8. University of Minnesota	4,995
9. University of Texas at Austin	4,821
10. University of California, Los Angeles	4,782
11. Harvard University	4,761
12. Michigan State University	4,521
13. Cornell University	4,343
14. Massachusetts Institute of Technology	4,310
15. New York University	4,106
16. Indiana University	4,096
17. University of Pittsburgh	3,894
18. University of Southern California	3,816
19. Purdue University	3,809
20. Pennsylvania State University	3,717
21. University of Washington	3,638
22. University of Maryland	3,613
23. University of Pennsylvania	3,468
24. Rutgers University	3,439
25. University of Chicago	3,214

SOURCE: *Digest of Education Statistics, 1990*, table 270.

Table 5.6

Fifty Largest University Research Libraries, 1990

Institution	Number of Volumes	Institution	Number of Volumes
1. HARVARD	11,874,148	13. WASHINGTON	4,908,988
2. YALE	8,862,768	14. MINNESOTA	4,651,111
3. ILLINOIS, URBANA	7,748,736	15. OHIO STATE	4,430,132
4. CALIFORNIA, BERKELEY	7,540,234	16. PRINCETON	4,276,086
5. MICHIGAN	6,369,490	17. INDIANA	4,133,331
6. TEXAS	6,265,236	18. DUKE	3,846,295
7. CALIFORNIA, LOS ANGELES	6,156,761	19. NORTH CAROLINA	3,751,660
8. COLUMBIA	6,032,545	20. PENNSYLVANIA	3,665,786
9. STANFORD	5,871,063	21. ARIZONA	3,549,281
10. CORNELL	5,216,501	22. NORTHWESTERN	3,474,423
11. CHICAGO	5,191,998	23. MICHIGAN STATE	3,417,388
12. WISCONSIN	5,036,144	24. RUTGERS	3,219,823

Institution	Number of Volumes	Institution	Number of Volumes
25. VIRGINIA	3,193,260	38. MISSOURI	2,486,014
26. IOWA	3,104,621	39. LOUISIANA STATE	2,460,219
27. PENNSYLVANIA STATE	3,095,863	40. SOUTH CAROLINA	2,431,129
28. NEW YORK UNIVERSITY	3,092,620	41. MASSACHUSETTS	2,409,946
29. FLORIDA	2,892,301	42. HAWAII	2,385,601
30. GEORGIA	2,889,108	43. CALIFORNIA, DAVIS	2,376,157
31. PITTSBURGH	2,878,713	44. WAYNE STATE	2,374,831
32. KANSAS	2,868,223	45. SYRACUSE	2,332,676
33. JOHNS HOPKINS	2,835,664	46. OKLAHOMA	2,297,087
34. ROCHESTER	2,686,996	47. COLORADO	2,286,736
35. SOUTHERN CALIFORNIA	2,626,271	48. WASHINGTON U.–ST. LOUIS	2,277,203
36. ARIZONA STATE	2,599,701	49. CONNECTICUT	2,271,849
37. SUNY–BUFFALO	2,591,006	50. BROWN	2,227,301

SOURCE: Association of Research Libraries, *ARL Statistics*, 1989–90, rank order table 1.

Table 5.7
Leading Research Universities, Public and Private
(institutions classified as Research Universities I by the Carnegie Foundation for the Advancement of Teaching, 1987)

Public Institutions

ARIZONA
    University of Arizona
CALIFORNIA
    University of California at Berkeley
    University of California at Davis
    University of California at Irvine
    University of California at Los Angeles
    University of California at San Diego
    University of California at San Francisco
COLORADO
    Colorado State University
    University of Colorado at Boulder
CONNECTICUT
    University of Connecticut
FLORIDA
    University of Florida
GEORGIA
    Georgia Institute of Technology
    University of Georgia
HAWAII
    University of Hawaii at Manoa
ILLINOIS
    University of Illinois at Chicago
    University of Illinois at Urbana-Champaign

INDIANA
    Indiana University at Bloomington
    Purdue University
IOWA
    University of Iowa
KENTUCKY
    University of Kentucky
LOUISIANA
    Louisiana State University
MARYLAND
    University of Maryland at College Park
MICHIGAN
    Michigan State University
    University of Michigan at Ann Arbor
MINNESOTA
    University of Minnesota at Twin Cities
MISSOURI
    University of Missouri at Columbia
NEW JERSEY
    Rutgers, The State University of New Jersey at New Brunswick
NEW MEXICO
    New Mexico State University
    University of New Mexico

Table 5.7 (cont.)

Public Institutions

NEW YORK
    State University of New York at Stony Brook
NORTH CAROLINA
    North Carolina State University
    University of North Carolina at Chapel Hill
OHIO
    University of Cincinnati
    Ohio State University
OREGON
    Oregon State University
PENNSYLVANIA
    Pennsylvania State University
    University of Pittsburgh
TENNESSEE
    University of Tennessee at Knoxville
TEXAS
    Texas A&M University
    University of Texas at Austin
UTAH
    University of Utah
VIRGINIA
    University of Virginia
    Virginia Polytechnic Institute and State
University
WASHINGTON
    University of Washington
WISCONSIN
    University of Wisconsin at Madison

Private Institutions

CALIFORNIA
    California Institute of Technology
    Stanford University
    University of Southern California

CONNECTICUT
    Yale University
District of Columbia
    Howard University
FLORIDA
    University of Miami
ILLINOIS
    Northwestern University
    University of Chicago
MARYLAND
    Johns Hopkins University
MASSACHUSETTS
    Boston University
    Harvard University
    Massachusetts Institute of Technology
MISSOURI
    Washington University
NEW JERSEY
    Princeton University
NEW YORK
    Columbia University
    Cornell University
    New York University
    Rockefeller University
    University of Rochester
    Yeshiva University
NORTH CAROLINA
    Duke University
OHIO
    Case Western Reserve University
PENNSYLVANIA
    Carnegie-Mellon University
    University of Pennsylvania
TENNESSEE
    Vanderbilt University

SOURCE: Carnegie Foundation for the Advancement of Teaching, *A Classification of Institutions of Higher Education*, 1987.

Table 6.1
Enrollment in Two-Year Colleges, 1989

Alabama (20)	69,881	Kentucky (30)	41,421	North Dakota (45)	7,960
Alaska (50)	289	Louisiana (37)	20,212	Ohio (8)	158,241
Arizona (9)	144,967	Maine (46)	7,720	Oklahoma (23)	62,670
Arkansas (38)	19,994	Maryland (14)	108,116	Oregon (17)	74,822
California (1)	1,048,842	Massachusetts (16)	9,213	Pennsylvania (7)	161,303
Colorado (18)	74,034	Michigan (6)	229,198	Rhode Island (40)	15,400
Connecticut (28)	45,943	Minnesota (21)	68,820	South Carolina (29)	43,988
Delaware (43)	9,957	Mississippi (27)	49,325	South Dakota (49)	359
D.C.	Not applicable	Missouri (19)	73,992	Tennessee (22)	65,420
Florida (4)	317,318	Montana (48)	5,968	Texas (2)	376,696
Georgia (24)	60,685	Nebraska (32)	32,799	Utah (35)	26,207
Hawaii (36)	20,533	Nevada (34)	29,122	Vermont (47)	6,898
Idaho (41)	13,561	New Hampshire (44)	9,480	Virginia (12)	131,635
Illinois (3)	350,039	New Jersey (13)	122,342	Washington (10)	144,918
Indiana (31)	38,102	New Mexico (33)	31,768	West Virginia (42)	13,032
Iowa (26)	50,725	New York (5)	265,071	Wisconsin (15)	95,975
Kansas (25)	56,856	North Carolina (11)	137,783	Wyoming (39)	16,824

SOURCE: *Digest of Education Statistics*, 1991, table 186.

Table 6.2
Proportion of Enrollment in Two-Year Colleges
(as a proportion of undergraduate enrollment, Fall 1989)

Alabama (21)	33%	Kentucky (34)	25%	North Dakota (40)	20%
Alaska (49)	01	Louisiana (48)	11	Ohio (27)	29
Arizona (3)	57	Maine (47)	13	Oklahoma (19)	36
Arkansas (37)	23	Maryland (10)	42	Oregon (8)	46
California (1)	60	Massachusetts (39)	21	Pennsylvania (32)	26
Colorado (18)	37	Michigan (12)	41	Rhode Island (40)	20
Connecticut (29)	27	Minnesota (29)	27	South Carolina (23)	30
Delaware (34)	25	Mississippi (10)	42	South Dakota (50)	01
D.C.	Not applicable	Missouri (29)	27	Tennessee (23)	30
Florida (5)	55	Montana (43)	16	Texas (9)	43
Georgia (34)	25	Nebraska (23)	30	Utah (37)	23
Hawaii (16)	38	Nevada (6)	52	Vermont (42)	19
Idaho (28)	28	New Hampshire (43)	16	Virginia (16)	38
Illinois (7)	49	New Jersey (14)	39	Washington (3)	57
Indiana (46)	14	New Mexico (14)	39	West Virginia (43)	16
Iowa (23)	30	New York (32)	26	Wisconsin (21)	33
Kansas (19)	36	North Carolina (13)	40	Wyoming (2)	58

SOURCE: Calculated from tables 178 and 184, *Digest of Education Statistics*, 1991.

Table 6.3
Average Enrollment at Community Colleges
(public two-year colleges, Fall 1989)

Alabama (43)	1,795	Kentucky (33)	2,498	North Dakota (47)	865
Alaska	Not applicable	Louisiana (27)	2,980	Ohio (23)	3,548
Arizona (4)	8,414	Maine (45)	1,256	Oklahoma (22)	4,052
Arkansas (44)	1,775	Maryland (10)	5,652	Oregon (9)	5,734
California (3)	9,721	Massachusetts (19)	4,722	Pennsylvania (12)	5,573
Colorado (20)	4,568	Michigan (5)	7,730	Rhode Island (1)	15,400
Connecticut (30)	2,604	Minnesota (35)	2,451	South Carolina (41)	1,876
Delaware (25)	3,319	Mississippi (38)	2,316	South Dakota	Not applicable
D.C.	Not applicable	Missouri (16)	5,091	Tennessee (21)	4,234
Florida (2)	11,153	Montana (48)	677	Texas (13)	5,554
Georgia (42)	1,805	Nebraska (34)	2,470	Utah (18)	5,036
Hawaii (24)	3,422	Nevada (6)	7,275	Vermont (36)	2,399
Idaho (28)	2,677	New Hampshire (46)	1,172	Virginia (14)	5,390
Illinois (7)	7,271	New Jersey (8)	6,234	Washington (15)	5,295
Indiana (32)	2,511	New Mexico (40)	1,986	West Virginia (31)	2,563
Iowa (26)	3,245	New York (17)	5,043	Wisconsin (11)	5,578
Kansas (29)	2,664	North Carolina (39)	2,287	Wyoming (37)	2,317

SOURCE: Calculated from tables 184 and 226, *Digest of Education Statistics, 1991.*

Table 6.4
Number of Associate Degrees Granted, 1988–89

Alabama (9)	15,322	Kentucky (27)	5,387	North Dakota (42)	1,875
Alaska (50)	603	Louisiana (37)	2,642	Ohio (8)	17,547
Arizona (22)	6,361	Maine (43)	1,859	Oklahoma (23)	6,204
Arkansas (38)	2,606	Maryland (19)	7,429	Oregon (30)	4,769
California (2)	48,353	Massachusetts (11)	13,316	Pennsylvania (7)	17,760
Colorado (24)	6,144	Michigan (6)	21,156	Rhode Island (33)	3,495
Connecticut (31)	4,721	Minnesota (18)	7,674	South Carolina (28)	5,202
Delaware (45)	1,288	Mississippi (29)	4,995	South Dakota (48)	791
D.C. (51)	403	Missouri (21)	6,909	Tennessee (25)	5,642
Florida (3)	33,718	Montana (49)	782	Texas (5)	22,828
Georgia (20)	7,389	Nebraska (36)	2,679	Utah (32)	3,750
Hawaii (41)	2,103	Nevada (47)	949	Vermont (46)	1,262
Idaho (34)	2,979	New Hampshire (39)	2,512	Virginia (16)	8,378
Illinois (4)	23,327	New Jersey (13)	9,935	Washington (10)	14,319
Indiana (15)	8,947	New Mexico (40)	2,455	West Virginia (35)	2,841
Iowa (17)	7,888	New York (1)	48,814	Wisconsin (14)	9,549
Kansas (26)	5,547	North Carolina (12)	10,647	Wyoming (44)	1,629

SOURCE: Table 14, "Less-than-4-Year Degrees and Other Awards in Higher Education, by Level of Award, Sex of Student, and State 1989–90," Office of Education Research, 1991.

Table 6.5

Associate Degrees Awarded per 10,000 Population, 1989–90

Alabama (1)	38	Kentucky (34)	15	North Dakota (5)	29
Alaska (44)	11	Louisiana (51)	6	Ohio (27)	16
Arizona (24)	17	Maine (34)	15	Oklahoma (16)	20
Arkansas (44)	11	Maryland (27)	16	Oregon (24)	17
California (27)	16	Massachusetts (12)	22	Pennsylvania (34)	15
Colorado (19)	19	Michigan (10)	23	Rhode Island (3)	35
Connecticut (38)	14	Minnesota (23)	18	South Carolina (34)	15
Delaware (19)	19	Mississippi (19)	19	South Dakota (44)	11
D.C. (50)	7	Missouri (38)	14	Tennessee (43)	12
Florida (9)	26	Montana (48)	10	Texas (41)	13
Georgia (44)	11	Nebraska (24)	17	Utah (12)	22
Hawaii (19)	19	Nevada (49)	8	Vermont (12)	22
Idaho (4)	30	New Hampshire (10)	23	Virginia (38)	14
Illinois (16)	20	New Jersey (41)	13	Washington (5)	29
Indiana (27)	16	New Mexico (27)	16	West Virginia (27)	16
Iowa (7)	28	New York (8)	27	Wisconsin (16)	20
Kansas (12)	22	North Carolina (27)	16	Wyoming (2)	36

SOURCE: Calculated from table 14, "Less-than-4-Year Degrees and Other Awards in Higher Education, by Level of Award, Sex of Student, and State 1989–90," Office of Education Research, 1991, and 1990 population table, U.S. Bureau of the Census.

Table 6.6

Tuition at Public Two-Year Colleges
(average undergraduate tuition, 1989–90)

Alabama (39)	$ 662	Kentucky (37)	$ 693	North Dakota (9)	$1,286
Alaska	Not applicable	Louisiana (25)	837	Ohio (2)	1,636
Arizona (43)	519	Maine (14)	1,134	Oklahoma (24)	840
Arkansas (40)	644	Maryland (11)	1,172	Oregon (34)	753
California (48)	112	Massachusetts (8)	1,332	Pennsylvania (5)	1,419
Colorado (32)	792	Michigan (16)	1,047	Rhode Island (17)	1,004
Connecticut (19)	915	Minnesota (4)	1,499	South Carolina (28)	807
Delaware (20)	882	Mississippi (38)	680	South Dakota	Not applicable
D.C.	Not applicable	Missouri (26)	815	Tennessee (29)	803
Florida (35)	729	Montana (21)	877	Texas (45)	455
Georgia (23)	852	Nebraska (18)	919	Utah (13)	1,136
Hawaii (46)	410	Nevada (42)	522	Vermont (1)	2,210
Idaho (33)	779	New Hampshire (3)	1,608	Virginia (27)	813
Illinois (22)	871	New Jersey (15)	1,130	Washington (31)	802
Indiana (7)	1,374	New Mexico (44)	496	West Virginia (29)	803
Iowa (10)	1,225	New York (6)	1,412	Wisconsin (12)	1,160
Kansas (36)	711	North Carolina (47)	288	Wyoming (41)	613

SOURCE: Digest of Education Statistics, 1991, table 292.

Table 6.7

Community College Tuition as a Proportion of Public Four-Year College In-State Tuition, 1989–90

Alabama (32)	44%	Kentucky (20)	53%	North Dakota (2)	80%
Alaska	Not applicable	Louisiana (26)	47	Ohio (8)	67
Arizona (38)	38	Maine (16)	57	Oklahoma (11)	64
Arkansas (26)	47	Maryland (19)	55	Oregon (35)	43
California (47)	9	Massachusetts (10)	65	Pennsylvania (32)	44
Colorado (35)	43	Michigan (37)	42	Rhode Island (32)	44
Connecticut (30)	45	Minnesota (4)	73	South Carolina (39)	37
Delaware (43)	32	Mississippi (39)	37	South Dakota	Not applicable
D.C.	Not applicable	Missouri (20)	53	Tennessee (16)	57
Florida	Not available	Montana (16)	57	Texas (26)	47
Georgia (22)	52	Nebraska (13)	61	Utah (2)	80
Hawaii (43)	32	Nevada (25)	48	Vermont (13)	61
Idaho (6)	70	New Hampshire (4)	73	Virginia (43)	32
Illinois (39)	37	New Jersey (30)	45	Washington (26)	47
Indiana (6)	70	New Mexico (39)	37	West Virginia (23)	51
Iowa (8)	67	New York (1)	97	Wisconsin (12)	62
Kansas (24)	49	North Carolina (46)	28	Wyoming (13)	61

SOURCE: Calculated from table 292, *Digest of Education Statistics, 1991*.

Table 6.8

Average Faculty Salary in Two-Year Colleges, 1989–90

Alabama (24)	$30,248	Kentucky (40)	$26,265	North Dakota (36)	$26,910
Alaska	Not available	Louisiana (38)	26,641	Ohio (19)	33,087
Arizona (8)	37,413	Maine (31)	28,659	Oklahoma (26)	29,210
Arkansas (44)	25,442	Maryland (5)	38,528	Oregon (21)	32,887
California (11)	35,442	Massachusetts (15)	34,394	Pennsylvania (14)	35,005
Colorado (33)	27,701	Michigan (3)	39,375	Rhode Island (9)	36,018
Connecticut (2)	40,576	Minnesota (7)	37,461	South Carolina (41)	25,890
Delaware (12)	35,401	Mississippi (37)	26,782	South Dakota (49)	21,000
D.C.	Not applicable	Missouri (20)	33,022	Tennessee (30)	28,698
Florida (17)	34,033	Montana (45)	25,255	Texas (22)	32,427
Georgia (25)	29,944	Nebraska (47)	24,404	Utah (35)	27,185
Hawaii (13)	35,317	Nevada (18)	33,409	Vermont (42)	25,491
Idaho (39)	26,323	New Hampshire (32)	28,407	Virginia (16)	34,209
Illinois (6)	37,916	New Jersey (4)	39,293	Washington (23)	31,435
Indiana (43)	25,477	New Mexico (34)	27,328	West Virginia (48)	24,127
Iowa (28)	28,973	New York (1)	41,292	Wisconsin (10)	35,501
Kansas (27)	28,978	North Carolina (46)	25,084	Wyoming (29)	28,961

SOURCE: U.S. Dept. of Education, *National Center for Education Statistics PEDS*, "Salaries, Tenure and Fringe Benefits of Full-Time Instructional Faculty, 1989–90" survey.

Table 6.9

Faculty Salaries at Two-Year Colleges as a Proportion of Salaries at Four-Year Colleges, 1989–90

Alabama (9)	88%	Kentucky (32)	77%	North Dakota (13)	84%
Alaska	Not available	Louisiana (29)	79	Ohio (23)	80
Arizona (9)	88	Maine (35)	76	Oklahoma (18)	82
Arkansas (31)	78	Maryland (7)	90	Oregon (2)	93
California (43)	70	Massachusetts (38)	72	Pennsylvania (17)	83
Colorado (44)	68	Michigan (1)	94	Rhode Island (23)	80
Connecticut (13)	84	Minnesota (2)	93	South Carolina (40)	71
Delaware (11)	86	Mississippi (20)	81	South Dakota (40)	71
D.C.	Not applicable	Missouri (4)	91	Tennessee (32)	77
Florida (12)	85	Montana (18)	82	Texas (20)	81
Georgia (23)	80	Nebraska (47)	67	Utah (44)	68
Hawaii (13)	84	Nevada (20)	81	Vermont (44)	68
Idaho (32)	77	New Hampshire (40)	71	Virginia (23)	80
Illinois (4)	91	New Jersey (13)	84	Washington (23)	80
Indiana (48)	65	New Mexico (36)	74	West Virginia (23)	80
Iowa (38)	72	New York (4)	91	Wisconsin (8)	89
Kansas (29)	79	North Carolina (48)	65	Wyoming (37)	73

SOURCE: Calculated from tables 10 and 11, *Salaries of Full-Time Instructional Faculty on 9- and 10-Month Contracts in Institutions of Higher Education, 1979–80 through 1989–90* (Washington, D.C. National Center for Education Statistics, 1991), pp. 15, 16.

Table 7.1

Adults with Four or More Years of College, 1989

Alabama (50)	11.6%	Kentucky (47)	14.9%	North Dakota (17)	22.2%
Alaska (14)	23.4	Louisiana (44)	16.6	Ohio (37)	17.6
Arizona (17)	22.2	Maine (33)	18.5	Oklahoma (40)	17.1
Arkansas (48)	14.8	Maryland (4)	27.4	Oregon (26)	20.2
California (8)	26.4	Massachusetts (2)	28.1	Pennsylvania (32)	18.6
Colorado (6)	27.0	Michigan (38)	17.3	Rhode Island (26)	20.2
Connecticut (3)	27.5	Minnesota (22)	21.5	South Carolina (44)	16.6
Delaware (30)	19.4	Mississippi (46)	15.6	South Dakota (34)	18.4
D.C. (1)	35.2	Missouri (21)	21.6	Tennessee (45)	15.7
Florida (28)	19.8	Montana (23)	21.1	Texas (20)	21.7
Georgia (36)	18.2	Nebraska (29)	19.7	Utah (10)	24.2
Hawaii (12)	23.9	Nevada (39)	17.2	Vermont (7)	26.7
Idaho (40)	17.1	New Hampshire (13)	23.5	Virginia (5)	27.3
Illinois (33)	21.1	New Jersey (9)	25.7	Washington (11)	24.1
Indiana (49)	13.8	New Mexico (25)	20.6	West Virginia (51)	11.1
Iowa (40)	17.1	New York (15)	22.8	Wisconsin (31)	18.9
Kansas (16)	22.3	North Carolina (35)	18.3	Wyoming (19)	21.9

SOURCE: *Educational Attainment in the United States, March 1989 and 1988*, Bureau of the Census, 1991, table 13, p. 89.

Tables 7.2, 7.3, 7.4, 7.5, 7.6
Educational Attainment of Various Groups by Region
(percentage of persons 25 years or older with four or more years of college, 1989)

| | All Races | | | Black | White | Hispanic Origin |
	Total	M	F			
Northeast	23.1	26.7	19.9	13.3	23.5	10.6
Midwest	18.9	22.3	15.8	11.3	19.2	12.3
South	19.3	22.3	16.6	10.3	21.0	12.0
West	24.8	28.3	21.5	18.6	24.4	7.6

SOURCE: U.S. Department of Commerce, Bureau of the Census, Current Population Reports, Population Characteristics Series P-20, no. 451, *Educational Attainment in the United States March 1989 and 1988* (Washington, D.C. Government Printing Office, August, 1991).

Table 7.7
Bachelor's Degrees Awarded per 10,000 Population, 1989–90

Alabama (28)	42	Kentucky (42)	33	North Dakota (5)	66
Alaska (50)	19	Louisiana (34)	38	Ohio (26)	43
Arizona (33)	39	Maine (32)	40	Oklahoma (26)	43
Arkansas (46)	32	Maryland (29)	41	Oregon (22)	44
California (42)	33	Massachusetts (4)	72	Pennsylvania (15)	51
Colorado (10)	53	Michigan (21)	46	Rhode Island (2)	88
Connecticut (22)	44	Minnesota (13)	52	South Carolina (34)	38
Delaware (10)	53	Mississippi (40)	34	South Dakota (13)	52
D.C. (1)	123	Missouri (19)	48	Tennessee (37)	36
Florida (49)	27	Montana (19)	48	Texas (37)	36
Georgia (42)	33	Nebraska (9)	55	Utah (6)	63
Hawaii (40)	34	Nevada (50)	19	Vermont (3)	80
Idaho (47)	31	New Hampshire (7)	61	Virginia (22)	44
Illinois (22)	44	New Jersey (48)	30	Washington (34)	38
Indiana (16)	50	New Mexico (42)	33	West Virginia (29)	41
Iowa (8)	58	New York (16)	50	Wisconsin (10)	53
Kansas (16)	50	North Carolina (29)	41	Wyoming (37)	36

SOURCE: Calculated from table 14, "Less-than-4-Year Degrees and Other Awards in Higher Education, by Level of Award, Sex of Student, and State 1989–90," Office of Education Research, 1991, and 1990 population table, U.S. Bureau of the Census.

Table 7.8
Master's Degrees Awarded per 10,000 Population, 1989–90

Alabama (25)	11	Kentucky (33)	10	North Dakota (33)	10
Alaska (49)	6	Louisiana (38)	9	Ohio (18)	12
Arizona (11)	14	Maine (49)	6	Oklahoma (15)	13
Arkansas (48)	7	Maryland (11)	14	Oregon (18)	12

California (18)	12	Massachusetts (2)	30	Pennsylvania (18)	12
Colorado (10)	15	Michigan (11)	14	Rhode Island (5)	18
Connecticut (4)	19	Minnesota (33)	10	South Carolina (25)	11
Delaware (18)	12	Mississippi (38)	9	South Dakota (25)	11
D.C. (1)	84	Missouri (8)	17	Tennessee (44)	8
Florida (44)	8	Montana (38)	9	Texas (25)	11
Georgia (33)	10	Nebraska (25)	11	Utah (11)	14
Hawaii (38)	9	Nevada (51)	5	Vermont (5)	18
Idaho (44)	8	New Hampshire (5)	18	Virginia (18)	12
Illinois (8)	17	New Jersey (38)	9	Washington (25)	11
Indiana (15)	13	New Mexico (18)	12	West Virginia (33)	10
Iowa (25)	11	New York (3)	21	Wisconsin (25)	11
Kansas (15)	13	North Carolina (38)	9	Wyoming (44)	8

SOURCE: Calculated from table 14, "Less-than-4-Year Degrees and Other Awards in Higher Education, by Level of Award, Sex of Student, and State 1989–90," Office of Education Research, 1991, and 1990 population table, U.S. Bureau of the Census.

Table 7.9
Doctoral Degrees Awarded per 10,000 Population, 1989–90

Alabama (41)	0.9%	Kentucky (41)	0.9%	North Dakota (33)	1.1%
Alaska (51)	0.1	Louisiana (36)	1.0	Ohio (15)	1.6
Arizona (19)	1.5	Maine (49)	0.3	Oklahoma (25)	1.3
Arkansas (47)	0.6	Maryland (10)	1.7	Oregon (15)	1.6
California (15)	1.6	Massachusetts (2)	3.5	Pennsylvania (10)	1.7
Colorado (3)	2.2	Michigan (22)	1.4	Rhode Island (8)	1.9
Connecticut (10)	1.7	Minnesota (10)	1.7	South Carolina (36)	1.0
Delaware (10)	1.7	Mississippi (33)	1.1	South Dakota (47)	0.6
D.C. (1)	8.8	Missouri (31)	1.2	Tennessee (25)	1.3
Florida (36)	1.0	Montana (41)	0.9	Texas (25)	1.3
Georgia (31)	1.2	Nebraska (19)	1.5	Utah (5)	2.1
Hawaii (36)	1.0	Nevada (49)	0.3	Vermont (36)	1.0
Idaho (41)	0.9	New Hampshire (45)	0.7	Virginia (22)	1.4
Illinois (5)	2.1	New Jersey (33)	1.1	Washington (25)	1.3
Indiana (8)	1.9	New Mexico (19)	1.5	West Virginia (45)	0.7
Iowa (3)	2.2	New York (5)	2.1	Wisconsin (15)	1.6
Kansas (22)	1.4	North Carolina (25)	1.3	Wyoming (25)	1.3

SOURCE: Calculated from table 14, "Less-than-4-Year Degrees and Other Awards in Higher Education, by Level of Award, Sex of Student, and State 1989–90," Office of Education Research, 1991, and 1990 population table, U.S. Bureau of the Census.

Table 7.10

Professional Degrees Awarded per 10,000 Population, 1989–90

Alabama (30)	2.1%	Kentucky (12)	3.1%	North Dakota (34)	1.7%
Alaska (51)	0.0	Louisiana (10)	3.5	Ohio (16)	2.8
Arizona (46)	1.1	Maine (43)	1.3	Oklahoma (13)	2.9
Arkansas (42)	1.4	Maryland (26)	2.3	Oregon (11)	3.3
California (19)	2.6	Massachusetts (2)	6.1	Pennsylvania (13)	2.9
Colorado (23)	2.4	Michigan (19)	2.6	Rhode Island (49)	0.8
Connecticut (13)	2.9	Minnesota (9)	3.6	South Carolina (34)	1.7
Delaware (4)	4.9	Mississippi (32)	1.9	South Dakota (38)	1.5
D.C. (1)	40.6	Missouri (5)	4.5	Tennessee (19)	2.6
Florida (34)	1.7	Montana (48)	0.9	Texas (23)	2.4
Georgia (16)	2.8	Nebraska (6)	4.2	Utah (29)	2.2
Hawaii (47)	1.0	Nevada (50)	0.4	Vermont (38)	1.5
Idaho (44)	1.2	New Hampshire (38)	1.5	Virginia (16)	2.8
Illinois (8)	3.9	New Jersey (26)	2.3	Washington (33)	1.8
Indiana (19)	2.6	New Mexico (44)	1.2	West Virginia (34)	1.7
Iowa (3)	5.1	New York (7)	4.0	Wisconsin (30)	2.1
Kansas (26)	2.3	North Carolina (23)	2.4	Wyoming (38)	1.5

SOURCE: Calculated from table 14, "Less-than-4-Year Degrees and Other Awards in Higher Education, by Level of Award, Sex of Student, and State 1989–90," Office of Education Research, 1991, and 1990 population table, U.S. Bureau of the Census.

Table 8.1

Total Costs at Public Colleges
(public four-year colleges and universities, 1989–90)

Alabama (39)	$4,119	Kentucky (41)	$4,047	North Dakota (28)	$4,360
Alaska (29)	4,352	Louisiana (32)	4,311	Ohio (9)	5,805
Arizona (10)	5,595	Maine (16)	5,429	Oklahoma (48)	3,754
Arkansas (36)	4,187	Maryland (2)	6,437	Oregon (23)	4,776
California (11)	5,547	Massachusetts (14)	5,478	Pennsylvania (4)	6,366
Colorado (22)	4,956	Michigan (8)	5,854	Rhode Island (5)	6,340
Connecticut (15)	5,445	Minnesota (24)	4,670	South Carolina (19)	5,089
Delaware (6)	6,196	Mississippi (34)	4,241	South Dakota (35)	4,236
D.C.	Not available	Missouri (40)	4,098	Tennessee (37)	4,172
Florida	Not available	Montana (20)	5,047	Texas (38)	4,168
Georgia (33)	4,308	Nebraska (44)	3,944	Utah (31)	4,342
Hawaii (26)	4,529	Nevada (43)	4,007	Vermont (1)	7,715
Idaho (46)	3,792	New Hampshire (13)	5,484	Virginia (7)	5,983
Illinois (12)	5,495	New Jersey (3)	6,396	Washington (25)	4,634
Indiana (21)	4,969	New Mexico (42)	4,018	West Virginia (17)	5,128
Iowa (30)	4,347	New York (18)	5,094	Wisconsin (27)	4,411
Kansas (49)	3,509	North Carolina (47)	3,790	Wyoming (45)	3,880

SOURCE: Digest of Education Statistics, 1991, table 292.

Table 8.2

Total Costs at Private Colleges
(private four-year colleges and universities, 1989–90)

Alabama (40)	$ 8,212	Kentucky (44)	$ 7,366	North Dakota (43)	$ 7,939
Alaska (35)	9,030	Louisiana (12)	13,464	Ohio (19)	11,330
Arizona (47)	6,432	Maine (7)	14,598	Oklahoma (41)	8,119
Arkansas (48)	6,110	Maryland (6)	14,621	Oregon (16)	12,074
California (9)	14,245	Massachusetts (1)	16,904	Pennsylvania (13)	13,416
Colorado (14)	12,920	Michigan (31)	9,764	Rhode Island (10)	14,126
Connecticut (2)	16,184	Minnesota (17)	11,891	South Carolina (37)	8,771
Delaware (36)	8,776	Mississippi (45)	7,208	South Dakota (38)	8,595
D.C. (5)	14,622	Missouri (24)	10,691	Tennessee (32)	9,642
Florida (23)	10,738	Montana (42)	8,013	Texas (33)	9,402
Georgia (28)	10,244	Nebraska (34)	9,101	Utah (49)	4,970
Hawaii (46)	6,997	Nevada	Not available	Vermont (4)	14,691
Idaho (30)	9,827	New Hampshire (3)	14,748	Virginia (27)	10,342
Illinois (15)	12,209	New Jersey (8)	14,439	Washington (20)	11,229
Indiana (18)	11,461	New Mexico (25)	10,563	West Virginia (29)	10,058
Iowa (22)	10,769	New York (11)	14,076	Wisconsin (21)	11,021
Kansas (39)	8,272	North Carolina (26)	10,412	Wyoming	Not applicable

SOURCE: *Digest of Education Statistics, 1991*, table 292.

Table 8.3

In-State Tuition
(public four-year colleges and universities, 1989–90)

Alabama (31)	$1,522	Kentucky (40)	$1,316	North Dakota (27)	$1,604
Alaska (43)	1,280	Louisiana (22)	1,768	Ohio (7)	2,432
Arizona (38)	1,362	Maine (16)	1,980	Oklahoma (41)	1,309
Arkansas (37)	1,376	Maryland (12)	2,120	Oregon (23)	1,738
California (44)	1,123	Massachusetts (14)	2,052	Pennsylvania (2)	3,210
Colorado (20)	1,830	Michigan (6)	2,484	Rhode Island (9)	2,281
Connecticut (15)	2,017	Minnesota (13)	2,063	South Carolina (11)	2,162
Delaware (3)	2,768	Mississippi (19)	1,858	South Dakota (24)	1,718
D.C. (50)	664	Missouri (30)	1,532	Tennessee (36)	1,406
Florida	Not available	Montana (29)	1,535	Texas (49)	959
Georgia (26)	1,631	Nebraska (32)	1,519	Utah (35)	1,429
Hawaii (42)	1,293	Nevada (46)	1,100	Vermont (1)	3,641
Idaho (45)	1,119	New Hampshire (10)	2,196	Virginia (4)	2,532
Illinois (8)	2,370	New Jersey (5)	2,511	Washington (25)	1,710
Indiana (17)	1,975	New Mexico (39)	1,326	West Virginia (28)	1,591
Iowa (21)	1,823	New York (34)	1,460	Wisconsin (18)	1,861
Kansas (33)	1,467	North Carolina (47)	1,015	Wyoming (48)	1,003

SOURCE: *Digest of Education Statistics, 1991*, table 292.

Table 8.4

Tuition at Private Colleges
(private four-year colleges and universities, 1989–90)

Alabama (37)	$ 5,484	Kentucky (46)	$ 4,689	North Dakota (41)	$ 5,149
Alaska (43)	5,078	Louisiana (13)	9,257	Ohio (20)	8,019
Arizona (47)	4,127	Maine (4)	10,425	Oklahoma (42)	5,133
Arkansas (49)	3,715	Maryland (7)	9,914	Oregon (16)	8,656
California (9)	9,489	Massachusetts (1)	11,450	Pennsylvania (11)	9,430
Colorado (14)	9,188	Michigan (32)	6,520	Rhode Island (6)	10,143
Connecticut (2)	11,268	Minnesota (15)	8,776	South Carolina (36)	5,914
Delaware (40)	5,388	Mississippi (45)	4,828	South Dakota (34)	6,224
D.C. (9)	9,489	Missouri (27)	7,170	Tennessee (31)	6,530
Florida (28)	7,153	Montana (44)	5,034	Texas (35)	6,047
Georgia (29)	7,076	Nebraska (33)	6,442	Utah (50)	1,975
Hawaii (48)	4,008	Nevada (39)	5,400	Vermont (3)	10,928
Idaho (30)	6,669	New Hampshire (5)	10,299	Virginia (25)	7,238
Illinois (17)	8,281	New Jersey (12)	9,398	Washington (19)	8,096
Indiana (18)	8,267	New Mexico (24)	7,335	West Virginia (26)	7,197
Iowa (21)	7,945	New York (8)	9,517	Wisconsin (22)	7,615
Kansas (38)	5,460	North Carolina (23)	7,373	Wyoming	Not applicable

SOURCE: *Digest of Education Statistics, 1991*, table 292.

Table 8.5

Ratio of Private to Public College Costs
(four-year institutions: tuition, fees, room, and board, 1989–90)

Alabama (31)	2.0	Kentucky (36)	1.8	North Dakota (36)	1.8
Alaska (29)	2.1	Louisiana (1)	3.1	Ohio (31)	2.0
Arizona (46)	1.1	Maine (5)	2.7	Oklahoma (26)	2.2
Arkansas (43)	1.5	Maryland (20)	2.3	Oregon (13)	2.5
California (8)	2.6	Massachusetts (1)	3.1	Pennsylvania (29)	2.1
Colorado (8)	2.6	Michigan (38)	1.7	Rhode Island (26)	2.2
Connecticut (3)	3.0	Minnesota (13)	2.5	South Carolina (38)	1.7
Delaware (45)	1.4	Mississippi (38)	1.7	South Dakota (31)	2.0
D.C.	Not available	Missouri (8)	2.6	Tennessee (20)	2.3
Florida (48)	0.0	Montana (42)	1.6	Texas (20)	2.3
Georgia (17)	2.4	Nebraska (20)	2.3	Utah (46)	1.1
Hawaii (43)	1.5	Nevada (48)	0.0	Vermont (35)	1.9
Idaho (8)	2.6	New Hampshire (5)	2.7	Virginia (38)	1.7
Illinois (26)	2.2	New Jersey (20)	2.3	Washington (17)	2.4
Indiana (20)	2.3	New Mexico (8)	2.6	West Virginia (30)	2.0
Iowa (13)	2.5	New York (4)	2.8	Wisconsin (13)	2.5
Kansas (17)	2.4	North Carolina (5)	2.7	Wyoming	Not applicable

SOURCE: Calculated from table 292, *Digest of Education Statistics, 1991*.

Table 8.6
State Spending per Student for Undergraduate Student Aid, 1989–90

State	$	State	$	State	$
Alabama (41)	16.08	Kentucky (17)	86.74	North Dakota (31)	34.18
Alaska (49)	8.29	Louisiana (39)	18.05	Ohio (15)	112.49
Arizona (43)	15.12	Maine (30)	35.23	Oklahoma (19)	76.49
Arkansas (26)	48.74	Maryland (22)	68.84	Oregon (21)	70.53
California (16)	98.95	Massachusetts (8)	175.21	Pennsylvania (6)	252.86
Colorado (25)	57.92	Michigan (14)	143.48	Rhode Island (11)	148.19
Connecticut (10)	148.23	Minnesota (5)	260.87	South Carolina (13)	144.73
Delaware (34)	26.74	Mississippi (45)	11.91	South Dakota (40)	17.47
D.C. (36)	21.55	Missouri (28)	45.60	Tennessee (23)	67.48
Florida (29)	39.05	Montana (44)	12.20	Texas (32)	32.32
Georgia (35)	22.72	Nebraska (37)	21.40	Utah (46)	10.45
Hawaii (42)	15.33	Nevada (51)	6.82	Vermont (2)	353.44
Idaho (50)	8.14	New Hampshire (38)	18.10	Virginia (33)	26.79
Illinois (4)	282.18	New Jersey (3)	316.05	Washington (24)	59.26
Indiana (9)	174.80	New Mexico (18)	79.53	West Virginia (20)	72.34
Iowa (7)	227.14	New York (1)	461.95	Wisconsin (12)	145.52
Kansas (27)	47.23	North Carolina (47)	9.89	Wyoming (48)	9.22

SOURCE: Calculated from table 301, *Digest of Education Statistics, 1991.*

Table 8.7
Grants to Students as a Percentage of State Tax Funds, 1990–91

State	%	State	%	State	%
Alabama (35)	1.8%	Kentucky (24)	3.2%	North Dakota (39)	1.1%
Alaska (37)	1.4	Louisiana (41)	0.8	Ohio (13)	5.3
Arizona (43)	0.6	Maine (28)	2.6	Oklahoma (11)	6.9
Arkansas (39)	1.1	Maryland (30)	2.4	Oregon (26)	2.8
California (27)	2.7	Massachusetts (4)	10.3	Pennsylvania (5)	10.2
Colorado (17)	4.7	Michigan (15)	5.0	Rhode Island (8)	7.5
Connecticut (9)	7.4	Minnesota (7)	7.6	South Carolina (25)	3.0
Delaware (36)	1.6	Mississippi (45)	0.4	South Dakota (43)	0.6
D.C.	Not applicable	Missouri (23)	3.4	Tennessee (30)	2.4
Florida (19)	4.2	Montana (47)	0.3	Texas (18)	4.6
Georgia (30)	2.4	Nebraska (42)	0.7	Utah (21)	3.9
Hawaii (49)	0.2	Nevada (47)	0.3	Vermont (1)	18.7
Idaho (45)	0.4	New Hampshire (34)	2.0	Virginia (30)	2.4
Illinois (3)	11.8	New Jersey (6)	9.7	Washington (28)	2.6
Indiana (12)	5.4	New Mexico (20)	4.0	West Virginia (16)	4.9
Iowa (10)	7.0	New York (2)	14.0	Wisconsin (13)	5.3
Kansas (37)	1.4	North Carolina (21)	3.9	Wyoming (49)	0.2

SOURCE: National Association of State Scholarship and Grant Programs, *22nd Annual Report, 1991,* table 22.

Table 9.1

State Appropriations per FTE Student at Public Institutions, 1988–89

State	$	State	$	State	$
Alabama (38)	$3,581	Kentucky (41)	$3,436	North Dakota (48)	$2,803
Alaska (1)	9,879	Louisiana (50)	2,598	Ohio (42)	3,423
Arizona (29)	3,882	Maine (9)	5,207	Oklahoma (35)	3,698
Arkansas (40)	3,497	Maryland (27)	4,011	Oregon (32)	3,789
California (10)	5,131	Massachusetts (8)	5,273	Pennsylvania (23)	4,068
Colorado (46)	2,941	Michigan (33)	3,766	Rhode Island (12)	4,671
Connecticut (4)	6,343	Minnesota (20)	4,231	South Carolina (31)	3,790
Delaware (13)	4,649	Mississippi (43)	3,343	South Dakota (44)	3,138
D.C. (2)	7,695	Missouri (25)	4,017	Tennessee (16)	4,396
Florida (11)	4,723	Montana (39)	3,502	Texas (45)	2,953
Georgia (19)	4,235	Nebraska (36)	3,632	Utah (25)	4,017
Hawaii (3)	7,458	Nevada (21)	4,085	Vermont (51)	2,337
Idaho (15)	4,416	New Hampshire (49)	2,782	Virginia (30)	3,876
Illinois (37)	3,595	New Jersey (6)	6,052	Washington (17)	4,274
Indiana (28)	3,893	New Mexico (14)	4,574	West Virginia (47)	2,918
Iowa (22)	4,073	New York (5)	6.309	Wisconsin (24)	4,028
Kansas (34)	3,725	North Carolina (18)	4,242	Wyoming (7)	6,028

SOURCE: *Statistical Almanac of the United States 1991*, 111th ed. (Washington, D.C.: U.S. Bureau of the Census, 1991), table 277.

Table 9.2

Proportion of General Expenditures Spent on Higher Education, 1988–89

State	%	State	%	State	%
Alabama (7)	7%	Kentucky (31)	5%	North Dakota (31)	5%
Alaska (49)	3	Louisiana (42)	4	Ohio (31)	5
Arizona (2)	8	Maine (31)	5	Oklahoma (19)	6
Arkansas (31)	5	Maryland (19)	6	Oregon (7)	7
California (2)	8	Massachusetts (42)	4	Pennsylvania (31)	5
Colorado (19)	6	Michigan (19)	6	Rhode Island (31)	5
Connecticut (42)	4	Minnesota (7)	7	South Carolina (19)	6
Delaware (31)	5	Mississippi (19)	6	South Dakota (31)	5
D.C.	Not available	Missouri (19)	6	Tennessee (7)	7
Florida (19)	6	Montana (31)	5	Texas (7)	7
Georgia (7)	7	Nebraska (2)	8	Utah (7)	7
Hawaii (7)	7	Nevada (42)	4	Vermont (50)	2
Idaho (7)	7	New Hampshire (42)	4	Virginia (7)	7
Illinois (19)	6	New Jersey (42)	4	Washington (19)	6
Indiana (19)	6	New Mexico (19)	6	West Virginia (42)	4
Iowa (7)	7	New York (31)	5	Wisconsin (7)	7
Kansas (1)	9	North Carolina (2)	8	Wyoming (2)	8

SOURCE: Calculated from *Statistical Almanac of the United States, 1991*, table 277, and State Expenditures table, Bureau of the Census, U.S. Department of Commerce.

Table 9.3

Increase in Public Higher Education Funding
(percent change, 1982–83 to 1987–88)

Alabama (10)	58.2%	Kentucky (28)	44.1%	North Dakota (42)	30.9%
Alaska (51)	3.9	Louisiana (44)	29.0	Ohio (20)	47.6
Arizona (25)	45.7	Maine (19)	47.8	Oklahoma (49)	13.0
Arkansas (11)	58.1	Maryland (23)	46.8	Oregon (35)	39.3
California (17)	48.6	Massachusetts (1)	79.8	Pennsylvania (14)	53.5
Colorado (36)	39.0	Michigan (16)	48.8	Rhode Island (32)	40.4
Connecticut (9)	59.5	Minnesota (15)	50.0	South Carolina (12)	57.8
Delaware (13)	53.9	Mississippi (41)	33.2	South Dakota (48)	16.3
D.C. (46)	24.2	Missouri (26)	44.7	Tennessee (2)	67.8
Florida (8)	59.7	Montana (47)	22.9	Texas (40)	34.8
Georgia (4)	63.7	Nebraska (38)	37.4	Utah (21)	47.2
Hawaii (42)	30.9	Nevada (4)	63.7	Vermont (18)	47.9
Idaho (33)	40.0	New Hampshire (24)	46.6	Virginia (7)	60.9
Illinois (31)	43.0	New Jersey (3)	65.4	Washington (26)	44.7
Indiana (22)	47.0	New Mexico (37)	38.1	West Virginia (50)	11.3
Iowa (39)	35.1	New York (29)	43.5	Wisconsin (30)	43.4
Kansas (34)	39.8	North Carolina (6)	61.6	Wyoming (45)	25.1

SOURCE: *Digest of Education Statistics, 1991*, table 322.

Table 9.4

Total Federal Funding of Higher Education
(federal obligations to colleges and universities, 1988, in thousands of dollars)

Alabama (21)	$ 249,118	Kentucky (34)	$ 124,882	North Dakota (43)	$ 54,401
Alaska (49)	23,955	Louisiana (27)	199,174	Ohio (11)	412,776
Arizona (28)	186,707	Maine (45)	38,712	Oklahoma (32)	127,973
Arkansas (37)	84,001	Maryland (5)	761,456	Oregon (29)	181,597
California (1)	3,420,059	Massachusetts (3)	1,110,075	Pennsylvania (6)	741,860
Colorado (24)	230,633	Michigan (9)	433,177	Rhode Island (38)	77,967
Connecticut (23)	231,478	Minnesota (22)	248,301	South Carolina (33)	126,927
Delaware (48)	27,618	Mississippi (31)	146,500	South Dakota (46)	35,883
D.C. (14)	307,405	Missouri (19)	254,409	Tennessee (20)	254,186
Florida (12)	358,838	Montana (47)	34,262	Texas (7)	720,480
Georgia (17)	299,505	Nebraska (39)	74,875	Utah (30)	163,120
Hawaii (41)	58,779	Nevada (51)	20,986	Vermont (40)	62,477
Idaho (44)	39,011	New Hampshire (42)	57,324	Virginia (18)	276,943
Illinois (4)	958,145	New Jersey (15)	306,764	Washington (13)	333,978
Indiana (25)	219,804	New Mexico (8)	710,830	West Virginia (36)	98,065
Iowa (26)	217,027	New York (2)	1,587,867	Wisconsin (16)	303,706
Kansas (35)	113,502	North Carolina (10)	412,890	Wyoming (50)	21,554

SOURCE: *Digest of Education Statistics, 1991*, table 345.

Table 9.5

Revenues from Federal Grants and Contracts
(per full-time faculty member, 1986–87)

Alabama (24)	$20,729	Kentucky (50)	$8,599	North Dakota (26)	$20,537
Alaska (14)	26,950	Louisiana (43)	12,446	Ohio (31)	16,250
Arizona (17)	24,204	Maine (42)	13,293	Oklahoma (46)	10,858
Arkansas (48)	9,668	Maryland (1)	44,740	Oregon (13)	27,387
California (4)	35,009	Massachusetts (3)	36,731	Pennsylvania (21)	21,942
Colorado (10)	30,234	Michigan (22)	21,714	Rhode Island (16)	24,496
Connecticut (9)	32,365	Minnesota (25)	20,568	South Carolina (41)	13,298
Delaware (32)	16,183	Mississippi (44)	12,151	South Dakota (39)	13,592
D.C. (11)	29,930	Missouri (29)	19,006	Tennessee (20)	22,544
Florida (33)	15,816	Montana (45)	11,753	Texas (34)	15,270
Georgia (30)	18,737	Nebraska (40)	13,495	Utah (2)	44,368
Hawaii (15)	26,282	Nevada (12)	28,814	Vermont (7)	32,963
Idaho (49)	9,313	New Hampshire (19)	23,297	Virginia (35)	15,062
Illinois (27)	20,021	New Jersey (37)	14,223	Washington (5)	34,640
Indiana (36)	14,747	New Mexico (8)	32,514	West Virginia (51)	8,326
Iowa (28)	19,284	New York (23)	20,914	Wisconsin (18)	23,706
Kansas (38)	13,991	North Carolina (6)	33,685	Wyoming (47)	10,588

SOURCE: *State Higher Education Profiles*, 3d ed. (Washington, D.C.: National Center for Education Statistics, 1991), table Q.

Table 9.6

Institutions with the Largest Endowments
(assets of June 30, 1991)

1.	Harvard University	$4,669,683,000	21. Johns Hopkins University	561,433,000
2.	University of Texas System	3,374,301,000	22. Rockefeller University	535,865,000
3.	Princeton University	2,624,082,000	23. California Institute of Technology	534,085,000
4.	Yale University	2,566,680,000	24. Duke University	527,635,000
5.	Stanford University	2,043,000,000	25. University of Southern California	522,931,000
6.	Columbia University	1,525,904,000	26. University of Virginia	507,002,000
7.	Washington University	1,442,616,000	27. University of Michigan	500,430,000
8.	Massachusetts Institution of Technology	1,442,526,000	28. Case Western Reserve University	442,722,000
9.	Texas A&M University System	1,395,454,000	29. Brown University	431,444,000
10.	Emory University	1,289,630,000	30. Macalester College	390,024,000
11.	Rice University	1,140,044,000	31. University of Delaware	389,523,000
12.	University of Chicago	1,080,462,000	32. Wellesley College	388,186,000
13.	Northwestern University	1,046,905,000	33. Southern Methodist University	366,566,000
14.	Cornell University	953,600,000	34. Ohio State University	351,238,000
15.	University of Pennsylvania	825,601,000	35. Smith College	343,133,000
16.	University of Notre Dame	637,234,000	36. Swarthmore College	342,453,000
17.	Vanderbilt University	613,207,000	37. Loyola University of Chicago	338,382,000
18.	Dartmouth College	594,582,000	38. Wake Forest University	336,361,000
19.	New York University	581,921,000	39. University of Cincinnati	329,176,000
20.	University of Rochester	578,358,000	40. Texas Christian University	328,624,000

SOURCE: National Association of College and University Business Officers, *Business Officer*, February 1992.

Table 9.7

Recipients of the Most Federal Funding for Research and
Development, 1989

1.	Johns Hopkins University	$411,879,000
2.	Stanford University	239,847,000
3.	Massachusetts Institute of Technology	207,157,000
4.	University of Washington	203,691,000
5.	University of California at Los Angeles	170,839,000
6.	University of Michigan	167,865,000
7.	University of California at San Diego	166,601,000
8.	University of California at San Francisco	159,027,000
9.	University of Wisconsin at Madison	150,474,000
10.	Columbia University	150,263,000
11.	Yale University	146,245,000
12.	Harvard University	141,760,000
13.	Cornell University	139,954,000
14.	University of Pennsylvania	132,805,000
15.	University of California at Berkeley	131,070,000
16.	University of Minnesota	128,727,000
17.	Pennsylvania State University	119,435,000
18.	University of Southern California	114,766,000
19.	Duke University	108,611,000
20.	Washington University	102,974,000

Source: National Science Foundation.

Table 10.1

Assessment, 1991
System-Wide Outcomes
(type of assessment requirement: state legislative body, state higher education board, or none)

Alabama	State board	Kentucky	State board	North Dakota	None
Alaska	State board	Louisiana	State board	Ohio	Legislative
Arizona	Legislative	Maine	None	Oklahoma	None
Arkansas	State board	Maryland	Legislative	Oregon	State board
California	None	Massachusetts	None	Pennsylvania	None
Colorado	State board	Michigan	None	Rhode Island	State board
Connecticut	State board	Minnesota	None	South Carolina	Legislative
Delaware	Legislative	Mississippi	Legislative	South Dakota	State board
D.C.	Not applicable	Missouri	State board	Tennessee	Legislative
Florida	Legislative	Montana	None	Texas	Legislative
Georgia	None	Nebraska	State board	Utah	None
Hawaii	Legislative	Nevada	State board	Vermont	None
Idaho	State board	New Hampshire	State board	Virginia	Legislative
Illinois	State board	New Jersey	State board	Washington	None
Indiana	None	New Mexico	Legislative	West Virginia	State board
Iowa	None	New York	State board	Wisconsin	State board
Kansas	None	North Carolina	Legislative	Wyoming	None

Source: Christine P. Paulson, *State Initiatives in Assessment and Outcome Measurement*. (Denver, 1990: Educational Commission of the States).

Table 10.2

Summary Map

Alabama (26)	1.7%	Kentucky (42)	1.5%	North Dakota (32)	1.6%
Alaska (20)	1.8	Louisiana (32)	1.6	Ohio (42)	1.5
Arizona (4)	2.1	Maine (50)	1.4	Oklahoma (7)	2.0
Arkansas (42)	1.5	Maryland (32)	1.6	Oregon (4)	2.1
California (16)	1.9	Massachusetts (7)	2.0	Pennsylvania (26)	1.7
Colorado (7)	2.0	Michigan (42)	1.5	Rhode Island (7)	2.0
Connecticut (32)	1.6	Minnesota (20)	1.8	South Carolina (26)	1.7
Delaware (4)	2.1	Mississippi (50)	1.4	South Dakota (26)	1.7
D.C.	Not applicable	Missouri (7)	2.0	Tennessee (16)	1.9
Florida (32)	1.6	Montana (42)	1.5	Texas (32)	1.6
Georgia (7)	2.0	Nebraska (32)	1.6	Utah (1)	2.3
Hawaii (16)	1.9	Nevada (42)	1.5	Vermont (20)	1.8
Idaho (16)	1.9	New Hampshire (32)	1.6	Virginia (7)	2.0
Illinois (42)	1.5	New Jersey (42)	1.5	Washington (26)	1.7
Indiana (26)	1.7	New Mexico (20)	1.8	West Virginia (32)	1.6
Iowa (3)	2.2	New York (20)	1.8	Wisconsin (7)	2.0
Kansas (20)	1.8	North Carolina (1)	2.3	Wyoming (7)	2.0

SOURCE: Compiled by the authors.

Sources

American Bar Association, Washington, D.C. Listing Of ABA-Approved Law Schools, 1991.

American Association of Dental Schools. *Admission Requirements of U.S. and Canadian Dental Schools, 1989–90.*

American Veterinary Medical Association. Listing of Veterinary Medical Schools, 1991. Schaumburg, Ill.

Association of Research Libraries. *ARL Statistics, 1989–90.* Washington, D.C.: Association of Research Libraries, 1991.

Business Officer, Journal of The National Association of College and University Business Officers. February 1992.

Carnegie Foundation for the Advancement of Teaching. A *Classification of Institutions of Higher Education.* 1987 ed. Princeton, N.J.: Carnegie Foundation for the Advancement of Teaching, 1987.

The Chronicle of Higher Education. Almanac. August 28, 1991.

Hispanic Association of Colleges and Universities. *Annual Report, 1990.* San Antonio, Tex.

Institute of International Education. *Open Doors 1990–91.* New York: Institute of International Education, 1991.

National Association for Equal Opportunity (NAFEO). Listing of Predominantly Black Institutions, 1990.

National Association of State Scholarship and Grant Programs. *22nd Annual Survey Report, 1991–1992 Academic Year.* Harrisburg, Pa.: Pennsylvania Higher Education Assistance Agency, 1991.

National Education Association. *Rankings of the States, 1991.* West Haven, Conn.: National Education Association, 1991.

National Merit Scholarship Corporation. *Annual Report, 1990–91.* Evanston, Ill., 1991.

Paulson, Christine P. *State Initiatives in Assessment and Outcome Measurement.* Denver: Educational Commission of the States, 1990.

Peterson's National College Databank. *The College Book of Lists, 5th edition, 1990.* Princeton, N.J.: Peterson's Guides, 1991.

Tribal College, The Journal of American Indian Higher Education. Vol. 3, no. 3 (Winter 1992).

U.S. Bureau of the Census. *1990 Census Profile, Race and Hispanic Origin.* No. 2, June 1991.

U.S. Bureau of the Census. *Statistical Abstract of the United States,* 111th ed. Washington, D.C.: U.S. Government Printing Office, 1991.

U.S. Bureau of the Census. *Current Population Reports, Series P-20, No. 451, Educational Attainment in the United States*, March 1989 and 1988. Washington, D.C.: U.S. Government Printing Office, 1991.

U.S. Bureau of the Census. Public Information Office Press Release, March 11, 1991, "Census Bureau Completes Distribution of 1990 Redistricting Tabulations to States."

U.S. Department of Education, National Center for Education Statistics. *Digest of Education Statistics, 1990.* Washington, D.C., 1990.

U.S. Department of Education, National Center for Education Statistics. *Digest of Education Statistics, 1991.* Washington, D.C., 1991

U.S. Department of Education, National Center for Education Statistics. *State Higher Education Profiles, 1991 Edition.* Washington, D.C.: U.S. Government Printing Office, 1991.

U.S. Department of Education, National Center for Education Statistics. *Trends in Racial/Ethnic Enrollment in Higher Education Fall 1980 through Fall 1990.* Washington, D.C., January 1992.

U.S. Department of Education, National Center for Education Statistics. *Salaries of Full-Time Instructional Faculty on 9- and 10-Month Contracts in Institutions of Higher Education, 1979–80 through 1989–90.* Washington, D.C., 1991.

U.S. Department of Education, Office of Education Research. *Less-than-4-Year Degrees and Other Awards in Higher Education, by Level of Award, Sex of Student, and State: 1989–90.* Washington, D.C., 1991.

U.S. Department of Education, National Center for Education Statistics PEDS. *Salaries, Tenure and Fringe Benefits of Full-Time, Instructional Faculty, 1989–90.* Washington, D.C., 1991.

Index